Martín de Porres,
Hero

CLAIRE HUCHET BISHOP

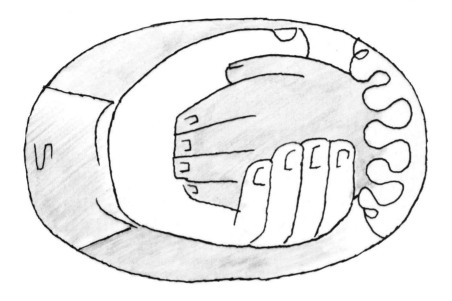

Illustrated by Jean Charlot

Martín de Porres, Hero

HOUGHTON MIFFLIN COMPANY BOSTON

Most grateful acknowledgement is due the Reverend Norbert Georges, O. P., General Director of The Blessed Martin Guild, Léon King, Editor of *Cross Currents,* and many other friends without whom this story could not have been written.

Contents

Claire Huchet Bishop, a French woman by birth and education, opened the first public library for French children, L'Heure Joyeuse, in Paris. Having inherited the gift of storytelling from her forbears, she told stories to the children who came to the library. Later, after she had married Frank Bishop, a talented American pianist, she came to New York to live, and became an American citizen. Once again she told stories in a library, the New York Public Library, and this time began to write them down.

Mrs. Bishop now has a wide following of readers from five years old to eighty. In addition to her two previous books on the lives of the saints, CHRIS-TOPHER THE GIANT, and BERNARD AND HIS DOGS, she has written an impressive list of best-selling books for children including: AUGUS-TUS; THE FERRYMAN; THE FIVE CHINESE BROTHERS; THE MAN WHO LOST HIS HEAD; BLUE SPRING FARM. A prize-winner in the New York Herald Tribune Spring Book Festival of 1947, PANCAKES-PARIS was a runner-up for the John Newbery Medal in 1948. In 1952 TWENTY AND TEN won the annual award of the Child Study Association of America, and in 1953 ALL ALONE was an Honor Book in the New York Herald Tribune Spring Festival.

The author of two adult books, Mrs. Bishop has contributed a number of articles to magazines published here and abroad. She lectures extensively, and has appeared in a weekly television program.

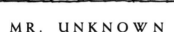

MR. UNKNOWN

YES, I HAVE!" shrieked Juana angrily, facing the
crowd of children gathered around her in the street. The
blue eyes of the little eight-year-old girl were ablaze, her
black curls all awry as she stamped her foot repeating defiantly: "I have! I have!"

"Liar!" shouted another girl. "You don't! You don't
have a father. Where is he, your father? Where is he?"

Juana tossed her curls back swiftly and yelled: "He went
on a journey!" A roar of laughter rose from the group of
children: "You bet he did!" they mocked. "Some journey!
Ah! Ah! Ah!"

"He did! He did!" screamed Juana hurling herself on the
group and starting to beat everybody with her fists. But
there were too many against her and soon she was bent
under the blows from all sides. "That will teach you!

That will teach you!" they shrieked, punching her, slapping her, tearing her apron, pulling her hair, scratching her face.

"Leave my little sister alone!" A shout, a command, a swift parting of the tormenters, and there stood a little boy who could not have been more than a year older than Juana. He was dark, with large black eyes, beautiful tight curly hair. He put his arm around Juana now in tears, saying soothingly:

"It's nothing Juana. Nothing. Really." And he kissed her and held her fast as if she were but a baby and he a strong, much older lad.

"Martín, take me home! Take me home, Martín!" wailed Juana.

"Oh, take me home, Martín! Take me home!" echoed the children giggling and starting to dance wildly around the pair and yelling:

> "Martín, take me home!
> My mother is a Negro,
> My father's eyes are blue,
> And his name is Mr. Unknown.
> Oh Martín, take me home!"

Martín drew himself up very straight, head high.

"Our father's name is Don Juan de Porres. My mother told me. He is from Spain. A nobleman . . ."

"Oh! Oh! Oh!" chuckled an old Indian passing by and stopping near the group. "Oh! Oh! Oh! That's a good one. A nobleman from Spain. Don't make me laugh, sonny. That's a real funny one! A nobleman *and* from Spain. Have not seen any such yet, and I should know: I was but a boy, fifty years ago, when they conquered this glorious

Inca land of ours which they call Peru. I have seen plenty
of these men from Spain, bloody, cruel, cheating, faithless,
greedy creatures. But a noble one? Nope. The name,
sonny, it has nothing to do with real nobility. What did you
say your father's name was?"

"He has no name," broke in an older girl. "Martín is
just making it up. A liar, like his sister. My mother, she
ought to know: she is Ana de Escarcena, Martín's god-
mother. She told me that when the priest baptized Martín he
said: Mother, Ana Velásquez, a free woman, father, unknown."

"Phew!" said the old Indian, and he spat on the ground,
shook his head and strolled away.

"See!" shrieked the children, closing in on Juana and
Martín. "Shame on you! We won't play with you! Why
do you come to us? You don't belong. Go and play with
your own kind, the people of your father, the nobleman from
Spain. We don't want you. Get out!" And a boy picked up
a stone.

Grabbing Juana's hand Martín started to run, pursued
by the yells of the children chanting:

> "Go back to your mother!
> She is a Negro.
> Go back to your father!
> He is a white man,
> A nobleman,
> Mr. Unknown!"

"Where have you been, the two of you?" shouted the
mother of the two children, as, all out of breath, they
stepped into the room. She gave a shriek as she noticed

Juana's torn clothes. Swiftly she marched toward Martín,. slapped his face, shook him by the shoulders, smacked him, yelling:

"So! That's the way you take care of your little sister! You good-for-nothing! Curse of my life! Take this! Take that! . . ."

Juana tried to squeeze herself between her mother and Martín in order to ward off some of the blows. "So you too!" screamed Ana Velásquez, roughly pushing aside the little girl. "What did I do to God to be afflicted with that pair of dark urchins?"

She suddenly let go of the children, her anger all spent, and wearily sat on the one stool in the room. She was a beautiful young Negro woman, but worries and bitterness had brought harshness into her eyes. She looked around sadly: the room was practically bare. The walls were made of a mixture of mud and straw. The floor, of beaten dirt, opened directly on the street with but a curtain as a door. There was a wooden table, three straw mats piled in one corner. An empty kettle hung from the hearth where no fire was lit.

Ana Velásquez's eyes came back to the two children, who had huddled together as far away from her as they could. She said sharply:

"It's all because of you both. All this (she made a gesture which took in the room), all this because of you. Why did you have to come into my life? I was doing fine with Don Juan de Porres, ever since the first time he met me, in Panama. He brought me here with him. He cared for me. Who knows? I might have become a grand lady, with a carriage, and horses, and a house of gold . . .''

"Of gold?" interrupted Juana softly, her blue eyes very wide.

"Of course, of gold," went on Ana Velásquez dryly. "All noble Spanish people in Peru have houses of gold. And your father, Juana, he was a nobleman, from Spain, from Castilla. A Castillán with blue eyes." She looked at Juana coldly. "I guess you have his eyes," she said. "And your skin is not very dark either. . . . Well, what's the use anyhow? The curse came first with this one." She pointed and snarled at Martín. "You just ruined my chance, that's what you did! From the time of your birth I was doomed. No carriage, no horses, no house of gold for me. Don Juan de Porres could not stand it: a child like you! So he left. And now . . ." She hung her head for a moment and then raising it swiftly she yelled to the children:

"Why are you staring at me like that? That's the truth. I did not want you. I did not! Do you get it? Well, now, take your mattresses and go to bed. Clear out!"

"I am hungry!" whimpered Juana.

"Can't be helped," answered her mother somberly. "I have no money. I have not been paid for the last week's laundry yet. Trust the rich to keep you waiting for your earnings. Tomorrow, Martín, you try to make yourself useful for once, and go and ask that great lady of Spain for the laundry money. Now, to bed. Both of you. And not another word. Get going!"

Martín lay on his mattress of leaves. He could not sleep. He was sore from the blows he had received. But, above all, he was sad. So sad that he felt as if his heart were about to

burst. At last tears came. They covered his little face like a curtain of water. They flowed, silently. He tasted their bitter savor on his lips and he put his fist in his mouth to prevent his sobbing aloud. He did not want to wake up his mother, or Juana. There, in the dark room, he felt so lonely that he was frightened. Around him there was no one to lean against, to cuddle to, no one to protect him, no one to soothe his grief. He was alone. Alone in the whole world. Stretched there on the floor, he felt emptiness all around him, in front, behind, on all sides. Alone, alone. In his distress he extended his arms for something to clutch, to hold. He longed for a kiss and a strong tender hug.

Juana stirred uneasily on her mattress and whispered: "Martín."

"I am here," answered Martín promptly and softly. But Juana did not say anything else. She had talked in her sleep.

Juana! thought the little boy. There was Juana. How much he loved her. His little sister with the Castilian blue eyes. She was his whole sunshine in this miserable life of his. Thinking of her he forgot his loneliness and fear. His tears dried up. He braced himself. He would always, always defend Juana. Just as he had done today. And when he was older he would fight those who dared annoy Juana. That he would do. He was strong. Very strong. He would show them. Everyone. His mother, and the children, and the Indian and the grandees of Spain, and Don Juan de Porres too.

Martín smiled at the dream and at last closed his eyes.

GOLD

HAND IN HAND, Juana and Martín skipped on Espíritu Santo Street where they lived. They were on their way to collect the laundry money from Dona Teresa. It was the middle of the morning and the air was still fresh and crisp; the swift river Rimac looked cooled, and in the distance rose the abrupt high peaks of the mountains, the Andes, covered with snow.

Lima was a truly American city. It was a young city, half a century old. It had no crooked streets like European cities; every thoroughfare was neatly laid at right angle. Rows of palm trees were planted along the avenues of the

well-to-do where houses resembled those of Spain, made of
stones, with carvings and balconies.

Espíritu Santo was a poor street. It did not have any palm
trees or stone houses. It was very narrow and without any
curb. Juana and Martín made a dash to the side to avoid
being run over by a carriage, with gold spiked wheels, which
suddenly came tearing down on the cobbled stones. The
children turned into the Plaza de Armas and made their way
slowly through the busy noisy market place: Indians
wrapped in their colorful shawls, Negroes with large
baskets marketing for some rich household, Spanish ladies
coming out of the Cathedral and wearing on their heads the
mantilla — a black or white lace kerchief — little gray
donkeys standing patiently next to the display of their
master's wares, and hordes of llamas, heads high, dignified
and somewhat disdainful, picking their way through the
crowd. The gold stirrups of Spanish cavaliers, the silver
shoes of their horses, flashed in the sun. Gold and silver
everywhere. Fabulous wealth of Peru, which for centuries
to come was to fire the imagination of European people.
Even today, in France for instance, when one wishes to
signify that somebody has found a quick way of making a
lot of money, people say: "It's Peru!"

Juana held tight to Martín's hand. There was such a
crowd, and so many wild children running in rags, and so
many Indians covered with sores and so many old ones begging. So much gold and so much misery. But there was
also the gay colorful display of goods. Juana loved it and
she said:

"Martín, I want to stay here."

"Not now, Juana. Later. When we come back. First we have to collect the money for the laundry. Then we can go marketing."

Leaving the market place they came to a stately mansion. It had no openings on the street, save some square heavily barred windows and a huge double door. Martín stood on tiptoe and lifted the gold hand-shaped knocker and let it fall. A dull sound boomed in the ears of the two children who stood there silent and a little afraid. Then the door opened as of itself. "Come," said Martín to Juana. They went in, and could not see a thing because their eyes were still full of sunshine and it was dark inside.

"This way," said a quiet voice behind them. And then they could see an Indian slowly closing the door. Martín recognized him, and apparently he, too, had recognized the little laundry boy. But now he hesitated, looking at Juana whom he had never seen before. Quickly Martín sensed the situation, and bending toward Juana he said:

"You wait for me here, Juana. I won't be long," and he hurried after the Indian.

Juana looked around. She liked the place: it was cool, and quiet. Far at the other end of the hall, she could see trees and flowers and birds flying to and fro. There were no doors and no glass, and slowly Juana made her way toward the garden. Now she could see a fountain shooting its spray in the midst of the foliage. She hurried along the hall, and suddenly she stopped: in the opening stood a little girl. She was taller than Juana and she looked even more so because she wore a long dress of stiff material, tight at the waist, billowing around her, and reaching down to the floor.

She had dark hair and dark fiery eyes and light skin. She looked surprised as she caught sight of Juana. Then she called, and her voice sounded like a command.

"Come here!"

Cautiously Juana came forward. She was wrapped in a scarlet piece of silk from a discarded petticoat of her mother; which had seen better days. But it was carefully arranged around her, and her hair was neatly combed and she was spotlessly clean. She looked very pretty, with her blue eyes and black curls.

"What's your name?" asked the older girl.

"Juana."

"Juana what?"

"Juana de Porres."

"De Porres!" cried the girl happily. "How wonderful! A grandee of Spain! I am delighted. Let us play. What would you like to do? Would you like to see my golden dolls? I have twelve of them. Would you like to see my gold dining set? Or perhaps you would like to see my dolls' casket of jewels, all silver and gold. Just tell me. What would you like?"

"That!" said Juana pointing to the fountain.

"Oh, how funny!" laughed the girl. "How funny! You are still a baby, aren't you?" She bent over and looked at Juana. "And you have beautiful blue eyes. Very blue. And this . . . dress . . . it is so nice. I wish I were dressed like that; then I could play and run." She pointed to her gold embroidered stiff bodice: "This gold is so heavy," she sighed.

"Gold?" inquired Juana, and slowly she touched the

material with one of her fingers and caressed it carefully.

"Of course gold," smiled the girl. "Oh, you are funny, and sweet. So sweet, you darling baby." And she hugged Juana tenderly. "I love you! I love you!" she cried. "Let's be friends. Tell me, how did you come here? I was so lonesome. How did . . ." She stopped suddenly and shrieked as she faced the entrance to the garden. "What's that? Who are you? How dare you? Get out! Get out! You horrible thing!"

Juana freed herself from the arms of the girl and looked. In the doorway stood Martín. She ran toward him.

"Come back here, you crazy baby!" cried the girl running after her.

"It's Martín! My brother," said Juana proudly.

"Your . . . brother. . . . a Negro . . ." stammered the girl. "But then . . . you . . ."

And suddenly she wheeled around and turned her back shouting in a rage: "Get out! Get out! Both of you. Get out! Go and play with your own kind, the Negro children. I don't want you. Get out. Get OUT!"

Juana let out a howl. Quickly Martín put his hand on her mouth. "Quiet," he ordered gently. Slowly, head high, without looking back once, he led her through the hall and out into the street.

Sobs heaved in Juana's breast as she trotted next to Martín. He did not say anything. He let her cry out her fill. Gradually she quieted down. Then he said gaily, clutching the laundry money in his hand: "Juana, what shall we buy at the market for dinner? What would you like?"

Juana did not answer. She pouted, resentful. After all,

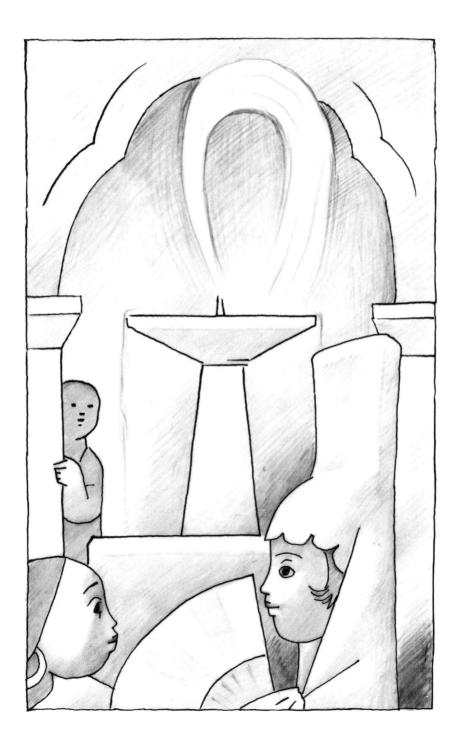

it was Martín's fault, wasn't it? Everything was going beautifully with the little Spanish rich girl until Martín appeared on the scene.

"What would you like?" repeated Martín patiently.

"I don't care!" she finally flung hotly. "I don't! Why should I? Last time we went shopping you gave away all the stuff we bought to beggars. That's what you did."

"Well, yes," admitted Martín sheepishly. "But, Juana, don't you remember? I had to do it. I had to. It was an Indian family, six little children and the mother was ill and the father had no work. They were terribly hungry."

"I was hungry too," said Juana darkly.

Martín stopped, bent and tried to kiss the little wet face, saying warmly: "Poor lamb! You have not forgotten. I did not mean you to go hungry. Honest, I didn't. You know that, don't you? I love you, I . . ."

But Juana closed her eyes and tightened her lips and struggled away from him. He straightened up sighing. "All right," he said finally. "Look, Juana, I promise, I promise you, I shall not give away anything, anything we buy to day. How is that, baby?"

All at once Juana opened her eyes, brushed the tears off her face and smiled. She could not bear Martín a grudge long. They were friends. They turned the corner of the street and were engulfed in the market shrieks.

"Señores, señoritas, see, see my beautiful yucas, figs, olives! All fresh, perfect!"

"Señores, señoritas, come, come! Dates and chirimoyas, sugary lucumas, capulís, oranges and raspberries. Blackberries from Urubamba, figs from Ica, grapes from the south, and Arequipa guayabas. Buy! Buy! Barato! Barato! Cheap! Cheap!"

"Stop here! This is the place for cacao from Cuzco, choclo and quina. Nowhere better than here. Stop here, señoritas!"

Everybody called, and the crowd jostled leisurely under the hot sun. Here and there, silent Indians stood next to baskets of fine wool from llamas, alpacas and vicuñas, or piles of tobacco leaves. These, like many other products, were entirely new to the Spanish conquerors of Peru. But to Juana and Martín who were born there, the market display had nothing unusual, except in so far that most of the time they did not have any money to buy anything.

But today was different. The laundry money was in Martín's hand. His mother had told him to do the marketing. And he had just promised Juana that he would not give away anything they would buy. Juana clasped her hands happily. "Let's buy everything! Everything!" she shrieked, jerking Martín's hand and jumping wildly in the midst of the crowd. Not watching where she was going, she stumbled against something and fell. She picked herself up almost at once, her hand still in Martín's. "Did you hurt yourself?" he asked. And as he said this he saw, at Juana's feet, an old Indian sitting on the ground, his back prone against a house. Juana had tripped on him. Juana shook her head vehemently: she was all right, and she pulled Martín away. "Come, come." But Martín stood there and said to the Indian: "Please, sir, excuse us. We did not mean any harm."

The piercing black eyes of the Indian rested on Martín.

Then he said slowly: "In that case, you will listen to my song."

Juana tugged at Martín's hand.

"A pleasure, sir," said Martín. He bent toward Juana and whispered: "We have to. We cannot offend him. It won't be long."

The old Indian gathered his shawl around him, and in a far-away and sad voice, thus, he began: *

> "In the days of the Ancients,
>   of the Ancients
>   of the Ancients,
>   when the last Inca was King,
>   ruling his land
>   with power,
>   with glory,
>   with majesty
>   since the beginning."

The old Indian stopped.

"What's an Inca?" asked Juana.

"Hush!" whispered Martín. "The Incas are Indians of royal blood."

"What's ro . . ."

But the singsong rose again:

> "To the Land of the Inca
>   there came men
>   of another land,
>   of another race,
>   of another color,
>   of another creed.
> They came to conquer the Inca.

* From *Secret of the Andes* by Ann Nolan Clark. Copyright 1952, by Viking Press, N.Y. (Reprinted by permission)

They came to subdue the people.
They came to rob their temples.
They came to destroy their gods."

Once more the Indian stopped. Juana did not understand
the song and she wished to go. But Martín seemed rooted
to the place. He was waiting breathlessly for the Indian to
go on with the story.

"Then the subjects of the Inca
sent gold to appease the enemy,
sent silver to soften the enemy,
sent emeralds to ransom their king,
sent rubies to set him free.
On the backs of ten thousand llamas
they loaded the wealth of the Andes,
they loaded the wealth of the Andes."

Then the old man was silent. Was it the end of the story,
Martín wondered, and dared not ask. He watched the man
slowly pulling himself up and steadying his back against the
wall. Probably the aged Indian had forgotten the end of the
tale. Suddenly the old man bent toward the children,
thrusting his head forward, and screamed:

"But the Spaniards killed the Inca!"

Juana gave a shriek and hid against Martín. There was
an angry murmur among the people who had gradually gathered together to listen. They started to argue vehemently
among themselves. But a Spanish soldier disengaging himself from the crowd walked to the old Indian, and with a
swift kick sent him sprawling on the ground. "That
settles it," he said to the crowd, making a gesture for them
to break up and move on, which they did at once. But
Martín, unnoticed, slipped behind him, holding Juana by the

hand, and ran to help the old man to his feet. Gently he made him sit down against the wall. The Indian had his eyes closed. With the corner of his shawl Martín tried to remove the dust from his face, pleading softly: "Grandpa, are you all right? Say something, Grandpa."

At last the old man opened his eyes, and seeing Martín, a flash of contempt spread on his face, and he pushed Martín away, saying sharply: "Slave!"

"I am no slave," said Martín. "My mother, she is a free woman."

"Makes no difference," retorted the Indian. "You are a Negro, and all Negroes are enemies of the Indians."

"Oh no!" cried Martín. "It cannot be! It's . . . It's . . . the Spaniards. You said it in your beautiful, beautiful song."

"Look, sonny," said the Indian, and his voice was kinder, "you seem to be bright. Just the same I can't explain to you the whole thing. You will have to grow up a bit more to understand what it is all about, if it ever can be understood. Now I can only say . . . Are you listening?"

"Yes, sir."

"This is what I tell you: you heard my song. The Spaniards killed the Inca, just as I sang, and they conquered the land and they took everything away from us. Then they enslaved us and sent us to work in the gold mines. It was a terrible life, and many of us died. So the Spaniards found that it was costing them too much. Then they brought Negroes who could stand working in the mines better than Indians. It meant that we Indians were left to starve. Perhaps it is a little difficult for a boy to understand. But that's what happened. First the Indians worked in the mines, they

were slaves and miserable, but some of them managed to sur-
vive. Now the Negroes work in the mines, and we, Indians,
we are free. Free to starve in our own country! How do
you like that, sonny?"

"I don't quite know what you mean," said Martín.

"Of course not," said the Indian gently. "I am just an
old man rattling along. You called me Grandpa, and right
you were. I have five little grandchildren. Their mother is
sick, and my son, their father, has no work. This is the
third day they have had nothing to eat. That's why I came
here. To sing and try to make some money. . . . But you
saw what happened."

"Let's go! Let's go!" pleaded Juana, tugging at Martín's hand.

"She is right," said the old Indian. "Run along, sonny. You are kindhearted but you cannot help it if your people took the bread out of my children's mouths. Keep to your own kind, whatever that is, because, as a matter of fact, the more I look at you and at your sister, the more I think that you have some of the blood of the white killer in you too. But that is not your fault either. Anyway there is nothing you can do for a poor old Indian and his starving family. Run along, run along!"

And the old Indian gathered his shawl about him, bent his head and shut his eyes.

Martín's small hand was on the Indian's bony fingers, pressing hard. "Grandpa," he said hoarsely and very fast, "for your grandchildren." Then he straightened up quickly saying, "Come, Juana," and he pulled her away and started to run.

They left the market behind, and soon they came to Espíritu Santo Street. Juana stopped short in her track:

"Martín? Did you . . . did you . . . give him . . . every . . . everything?"

Martín shook his head up and down slowly.

"Oh Martín!" wailed Juana. Tears came up to her eyes and Martín looked away. He could not stand it. But suddenly he felt her small arms around him as she said passionately: "*We* had to! *We* had to! Did not *we*, Martín? *We* just had to."

They stood for a while holding each other fast, and then, slowly, very slowly, they made their way toward home.

THE SCUM OF THE EARTH 3

MARTÍN was kneeling on the floor of the Church of Santo Domingo, the church he liked best. He was sore all over from yesterday's beating. His head rested on his folded arms. At first he knew nothing but the ache of his body. But gradually the coolness, quietness and darkness of the place made him feel better. He sat on his heels and said in his heart: Lord, it is too difficult. I am hungry. Juana is hungry. The Indian grandchildren were hungry. But Juana and I, we had eaten once the day before. The Indians . . . it was three days. And I had the money. . . . But my mother, she worked very hard to earn that money. My mother, she says that it was no money to feed the Indians with. But then, who is going to feed them? Oh, Lord, I don't know. . . . I don't know what to do. It is too difficult. Too difficult.

And with his grief, his physical ache came back and also the pangs of hunger, and he sat there doubled up in pain, pain within and without, and he wished desperately that someone would come and lift him out of his misery. As far as he could remember, it had always been thus: loneliness, hunger, beatings. He was not wanted at home. He never belonged. Anywhere. At the most he was just tolerated in the world. "Oh, Santa María, will no one ever come? Will no one ever come?"

Gradually he quieted down. Slowly he went out. The sun was pouring out on the plaza. He sat near the gutter and watched the water flowing on the cobblestones. He spied an ant running back and forth, wishing evidently to get across. "Poor little thing!" said Martín. "You cannot swim. You are out of luck. Just like me. Wait!" He looked around, snatched a twig in the dust and set it in front of the ant, like a bridge over the water. "There!" he said, and crouched to see what would happen. In no time at all the ant had discovered the bridge, crossed it and was on its way on the other side. Martín clapped his hands joyously. "See, little ant! When I grow up I am going to look after all those who are out of luck: the poor, the sick, the old, the Indians, the Negroes, the girls, the boys *and* the animals. EVERYBODY!" He laughed, took a deep breath, got up and strutted in a grand manner as if he had a sword at his side and a plumed hat on his head. He, Martín, would make everybody happy.

What was happening? Everybody running and screaming on the square: "A boat has arrived! From Spain!" Oh, my! He took to his heels and ran all the way home: "Juana! Juana! Come quick! A boat has arrived from Spain. Mother, may she come?"

"Yes, but don't stay long. I shall have some clean laundry for you to take to a customer. Here is a hunk of bread for both of you."

How good the bread tasted! Back on the plaza, the two children mingled with the crowd to hear the news: "The boat docked at Callao during the night. . . . Those on board must be on their way now. . . . The Governor has sent plenty of carriages and horses. . . . Lima is only two leagues (eight miles) from the harbor of Callao, they will be here any minute now. . . . I hope my husband is there. Have not heard from him for a year. Spain is so far away. . . . How long do you suppose it took that boat to come? Two months? . . . I hope my father is there. . . . I hope there is news from my son. . . ."

Martín and Juana did not expect anyone but they were just as excited as anybody else when the cry rose: "Here they are! Here they are!"

In a cloud of dust they rode into Lima, horses' manes flying in the wind, their silver hoofs flashing in the sun, the men's silver helmets shining like mirrors and their richly ornate waistcoats and breeches shimmering in the light. They flung themselves off their horses, immediately surrounded by the cheering, laughing and weeping crowd, kissed, hugged, caressed, and led away by women and children. Just one man did not seem to be in a hurry to go anywhere. Apparently no family had been waiting for him. Martín, watching with Juana, began to feel sorry for the Spaniard. He looked very grand and regal, standing there all by himself in his beautiful costume, his sword dangling at his side. But just then a man on horseback, wearing the livery of the Governor, rode briskly onto the plaza, dismounted quickly near the lonely knight, bowed low and said:

"His Excellency the Governor begs the Knight of Alcantara to do him the honor of accepting his hospitality."

Martín felt glad. So after all, the knight was not alone. He had a place to go. And what a place! The Governor's house, no less! That man must be very important to be invited there. What was his name? Knight of Alcantara. Alcantara. Alcantara. Martín said the word over and over again. He loved new, strange words. And this was such a good one to fill one's mouth and roll on the tongue. Alcantara!

"Martín?"

"Yes, Juana."

"That man . . . the one alone . . . He had blue blue eyes. Did you see? Blue, blue, blue. Just like mine."

It was late in the evening. The Knight of Alcantara sat in the Governor's patio with his host. They had dined on magnificent food and drunk costly wines. The Governor knew when he was entertaining someone whose star was rising.

The Knight of Alcantara had given him news of his family in Spain and also of the political situation in the Old World. And now it was the Governor's turn to speak of Lima, the

City of Kings, the proudest Spanish possession, the capital of the entire New World.

"When you think of it," he said, "it seems quite unbelievable, really, that our Lima was founded only fifty-two years ago, in 1535. That it was entirely built by Pizarro who but a little over half a century ago had discovered this land of Peru. Pizarro and his handful of men who had heard of a fabulous country where everything was made of gold. And they sailed along that unknown coast and happened to hit on the right spot. One hundred and seventy men, seventy horses and three arquebuses to conquer an Empire! Oh, of course, as we well know, Pizarro had to trick, cheat, betray, kill and murder the natives right and left. But he survived. A real Spaniard. A great man. That is, of course, for us Spaniards. Here, the Indians call him a sinister scoundrel, a man without honor, a killer."

"It is unfair of the Indians to speak thus," said the Knight of Alcantara. "After all, most of them are still alive even if in a precarious condition. They have not been exterminated. And besides, when everything is said against Pizarro, it still remains that it is through him that the blessings of Christian civilization were brought to this land."

"I don't know," said the Governor slowly, "I don't know. ... Of course, you recall that in the Indian way of life here, before we came, no one was ever left in need; they had a system whereby everybody ate and had a roof. Now, when one sees, as I do, the tremendous Spanish prosperity, and on the other hand the misery, squalor, disease, which afflict the natives ... one wonders ..."

"My dear Governor," broke in the Knight of Alcantara

coolly, "may I remind you that it is unhealthy to 'wonder' in those matters. The Holy Office of the Inquisition is expert at dealing with those un-Spanish, I mean, un-Christian, statements. But, of course," he added in a more friendly voice, "you did not mean it that way. However, even in a jest it is better to be careful not to incriminate yourself."

"Yes, yes, of course," said the Governor hastily. "You are quite right. Anyway I have not asked you here tonight to burden you with the care of the office I have the privilege to hold in behalf of His Most Christian Majesty. As a matter of fact the office is a source of real joy, and sometimes in the most unexpected way. You will hardly believe it if I tell you that, now, what cheers me no end is a little Negro boy."

The Knight arched his brow: "You mean . . . a jester, a slave you have around? I would be delighted to see his pranks."

"No, my dear Knight, nothing of that sort. Let me explain. There is now, in our good city of Lima, a little Negro boy, an eight-year-old child, who is a marvel."

"A marvel?"

"Of goodness."

"Oh my dear Governor!" chuckled the Knight. "I hardly expected such pious words from you."

"Why not? You may not be aware of it, but I have always been religious. That is, I strongly believe in what the Church teaches . . ."

"I hope so," interrupted the Knight somewhat dryly.

"Well, my dear Knight, the little chap I am telling you about does it."

"Does what?"

"What the Church says Christ taught: to help others, the poor, the sick, the old, the lonely."

Now the Knight of Alcantara was laughing right out loud.

"Excuse me, excuse me! But this is too funny, Excellency! Just as if the religious orders had not been doing that very same thing for ages, and right here too of course."

"I know about the work of the religious orders," said the Governor. "But this little boy, it's the way he does it. I cannot explain. It's the way . . ."

"And I suppose," went on the Knight gaily, "your paragon is like all very good children, a frail boy, a little sickly, and so, so sweet. Phew! He bores me!"

"But not at all! Not at all!" the Governor roared suddenly, bringing his fist down on the table. "He is just a regular eight-year-old lad, full of fun and mischief. But what a heart! He gives away everything."

"How come? A rich family?"

"No, no, very poor. He gives whatever he has. He is always helping. Everybody. Animals too. It must seem queer to you my talking this way, but wait until tomorrow and you will soon find out that everybody in town is talking about that little boy."

"He will become a prig," snapped the Knight.

"I don't think so, and anyway I don't believe he knows that people talk about him, which of course is much better. I personally have never met him, but I know of him, and it does me good. I will tell you: sometimes it makes me feel that all is not lost here, in Peru. That, after all, when we came here . . ." He hesitated, and then looked the Knight of Alcantara straight in the eyes. "That when we came here, we did not trade Christ for the gold of the Incas."

"We?" exclaimed the Knight of Alcantara. "But you were speaking of a Negro."

"I know," said the Governor quietly. "I have even heard it said that he is not pure Negro. He is a half-breed, a mixed blood. Negro *and* Spanish, if you please, my dear Knight of Alcantara. And as you know, *that* is the scum of the earth."

ARTÍN ran aft on the boat. The sails billowed
under the wind. The boat bounced on the waves and Martín,
delighted, took long slides on the slippery deck. Salt was on
his lips, wind in his quivering nose and his body responded
to the thrill of keeping his balance on the rocking ship. A
sudden lurch threw him roughly against the railing. He
laughed and raised his head as he heard a call. Up above
him, there was the captain at the wheel, and standing next
to him, the Knight of Alcantara. The latter waved at
Martín, cupped his hands and shouted:

"Where is Juana?"

"Sick, in her cabin," called back Martín grinning.

"Better get inside, yourself," called the Knight of Alcantara. "The sea is getting rough."

Martín nodded, and at once made his way toward the covered part of the boat.

The Knight of Alcantara! The handsome man he and Juana had watched on the plaza as he was being approached by the Governor's messenger. And here they were now, he and Juana, on a boat with this Knight of Alcantara. It was like a story, a dream. Was it really, really true? It was. Could he ever forget how it happened?

He was coming back by himself from the market. He was going slowly. Not that he had anything to carry, but his feet were heavy, because "he had done it again." A woman had held a sickly child in her arms, and waited for alms. Martín had just completed the purchase his mother had sent him to make. He was holding an old hen and had an armful of vegetables. Such a treat! Already he could taste the delicious broth, the fragrance of the long-cooked fowl and vegetables. Martín and his family had not had such a meal for months. And suddenly he had met the eyes of the woman beggar with the sick baby in her arms. She had not uttered a word, nor made a gesture. It was the way she had looked at Martín. Her eyes said: This hen and vegetables, that will save my child's life. It was so plain, so clear. Martín did not even have to think about it. Without a moment's hesitation he had thrust the whole thing into her arms, just as if it actually belonged to her, and it did, at least that was the way Martín felt. Then he had turned away swiftly, almost running into a man. As he walked slowly on Espíritu Santo Street he heard footsteps behind him. He looked back and saw in the distance a man whom he recognized at once: it was the Knight of Alcantara. And then suddenly he remembered that this was the same man whom he had almost bumped a few minutes before on the market place. The Knight was there watching when Martín gave the hen to the woman. And gradually it seemed to Martín that within those last days he had run into the Knight of Alcantara over and over again, everywhere in town. And now here was the Knight once more, and in such a street. What could an elegant gentleman do in these slummy quarters?

After that, everything had gone very fast. Martín got home, and this time his mother reached for a whip. She was shouting, Juana was shrieking "No! No!" Martín protecting his head with his arms was trying to steel himself against the first blow. The whip hissed in the air, and at that very moment there was a sharp call: "Ana!" The whip never struck, and for an instant there was a dead silence in the room. Then a wild happy cry from Ana Velásquez. Martín cautiously peered from under his raised folded arms. And there, in the entrance, stood the Knight of Alcantara. And in the next moment, to Martín's utter bewilderment, his mother had flung herself in the arms of the Knight, sobbing: "Oh Juan! Juan de Porres!"

"And so this is my son Martín," said the Knight of Alcantara as later he sat on the one stool and patted Martín on the shoulder. Martín's head whirled. His father! Don Juan de Porres. The Knight of Alcantara!

What happened next was all a blur. There were moments of sheer happiness, with plenty to eat and no beatings what-

soever. His mother laughed and took time out from her
work. The Knight, his father, came and made short quick
visits during which Martín's mother pleaded with him over
and over again to take her with him, and he always answered:

"It cannot be done, Ana. It cannot be done." Then she
would weep. And one day, after they had said the same thing
over and over again, Martín had heard his father say: "I told
you, Ana, I cannot take you with me, and that is final. But
I'll tell you what I can do: I will take the children with me

to Guayaquil where my uncle lives. And there I can see them and they can be given a good education. They should do well. Martín is very clever and Juana is pretty. They will be off your hands and you won't have to worry about them any more."

Martín was thrilled, but also a little sad. He wished his mother could come too, especially as time went on and Ana Velásquez kept telling him, "Oh, Martín, what shall I do without you? I was awfully harsh with you. But you must understand. I had to. I was only a poor woman, all alone, and you had such outlandish ideas. I was trying to put some sense in your head. I was working so hard to bring you up, you and Juana, and when a woman is alone, and poor . . ."

Martín tried to cheer her up: "I'll come back, Mother. Then I'll be a big man. And I'll take care of you. Just wait and see!"

"You will forget me," Ana would say sadly.

"No, I won't," would answer Martín. And he meant it.

And now here he was, on his way to Guayaquil in Ecuador, with the Knight of Alcantara, Don Juan de Porres, his father.

He ran to the hammock where Juana lay. "Feeling better?" he inquired tenderly.

"A little," she said.

He sat on the floor and said: "Listen, Juana. Someone did come after all." Juana did not exactly know what Martín meant. She did not know that he was thinking of the time when he had wished so desperately for someone to come and pull him out of his misery. But she guessed that probably he was talking about their long lost father.

"Yes," she answered softly, "he did come. And, after

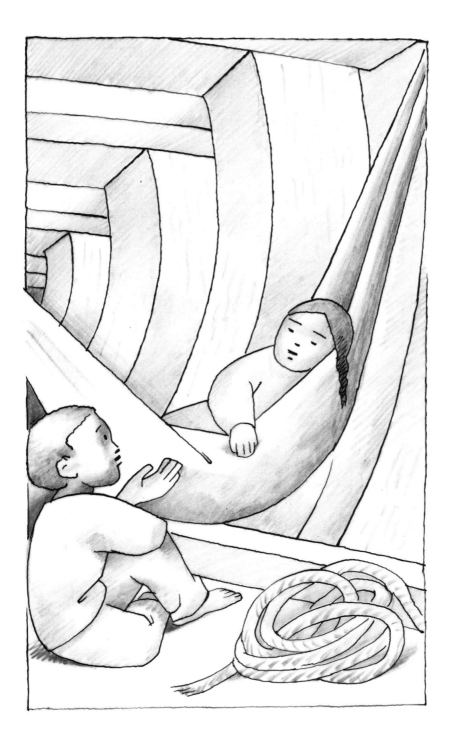

all, I *did* tell the truth to the girls, did I not, Martín? We did have a father. And," she added, her eyes shining, "there, in the trunk, I have such pretty dresses!"

"And who are those children?" asked Don Diego de Miranda, knitting his brow.

"My children," said Don Juan de Porres, "and your nephew and niece, my dear uncle."

"Your . . . ??"

Don Juan de Porres nodded quietly. In the richly decorated room of the mansion of Don Diego, in Guayaquil, everything stood still. At last Don Diego asked: "How old are they?"

"Seven and eight," said Don Juan de Porres.

Don Diego eyed the two children standing in front of him. "The baby is pretty," he said. "She has your eyes, Juan. The boy . . . What is your name, boy?"

"Martín de Porres," said Martín slowly, drawing himself up. Don Diego burst out laughing and gave a poke of the elbow to Juan de Porres who stood next to him. "Somebody has got Spanish dignity and fire all right! My! Too bad that . . ."

Don Juan de Porres leaned quickly and whispered behind his hand: "Martín is very intelligent, and so goodhearted. Why, when I arrived in Lima, the whole town was buzzing about his kindness. And I did not know it was my son they were talking about. I did not even know what my son looked like. I have been away so long. And you can imagine . . . Everything so complicated. . . . I was at a loss at first, that is, when I found out. It was quite a blow to me.

I had sort of . . . dismissed the whole affair from my mind."

"I understand," said Don Diego. "We in the New World are a forgetful lot. Well, what do you want me to do?"

Juan de Porres straightened up and said aloud: "Dear Uncle, it is my wish that these children be educated properly. I have no time to see to it. I was hoping that you might be willing to undertake it. Or is that too much to expect?"

"No, it is not. They can stay here with me. Juana can be taught all about woman's household duties and I could get a tutor for Martín. And you could visit with them whenever you had time."

Happy were those years in the house of Don Diego de Miranda. No hunger, no beating. From time to time, glimpses of his father, and the thrill of discovering so many interesting things through his teacher. Martín was given an education far above that of the average children of any nation or race at the time. He learned to read, write, count, and he learned fast. But what he liked best was to hear about the human body, animals and plants. He could study plants right in his uncle's garden. There were animals there too, and it was not long before Martín had made friends with cats and dogs, birds, turtles and lizards. As to insects, how fascinating it was to watch them, lying on one's tummy, for hours. He was very careful not to harm anything. He spoke to flowers and skipped over spiders which happened to cross his path. He was full of curiosity about everything. He played a lot too. And he was growing into a sturdy and strong boy.

About two years of paradise in Guayaquil, free from hunger and fear. Gone were the slum, the squalor, the beating, the spite, the misery without and within. Martín was out of it all.

He was. But in Lima, in the City of Kings, there were still thousands and thousands who were not. They did not have a Knight of Alcantara to rescue them, even for a short time. There could not be a Knight of Alcantara to everybody out of luck, to all the poor, the sick, the exploited, the unwanted, the orphans, the old, the despised. Then what? What did it matter that once a little boy, a mixed blood, an outcast, had been lifted out of the pit through a tardy and fitful remorse (or was it just a whim?) of one Spanish conqueror? What difference did it make to all the wretched people in Lima?

Martín could not forget Lima: "Someday I will go back and help everybody."

It seemed a long way off, but in the New World life always moved fast, and one day Don Juan de Porres, came in, radiant: he had been appointed Governor of Panama. Such an honor, such a distinguished situation, and also, of course, such a profitable one.

"I cannot take the children with me," he said to his uncle. "How would it look? . . . You know what I mean."

"They can remain here," said the uncle. "Juana can be sent to a finishing school in a convent, and Martín can go on with his studies. His teacher tells me he is very gifted, quite advanced for his years. He is an endearing little chap anyhow, though quite stubborn I am afraid. Why not tell him about the new situation and see what he has to say?"

They did. "Well, Martín, you will be eleven years old

soon. Have you ever given a thought to what you would like to do?"

"Help people," said Martín at once. "Help people. Feed them. Cure them. Look after them. Everything."

"That is a big order. Perhaps then the best way to start is to study medicine. What do you say?"

Martín's eyes shone.

Then they explained to him about Don Juan de Porres's new appointment in Panama, and how the uncle was willing for Martín to stay with him in Guayaquil to study. Martín listened quietly and when they had finished he said:

"Please forgive me. But if my father goes away for good, then I do not want to stay here. I want to go back to my mother."

"To your mother!" they cried in astonishment. How could he say such a thing? Had he forgotten what it was like to be there?

He had not at all, though he did not say so. As a matter of fact he was never to forget those eight miserable years of his childhood in Lima. But to his father and uncle he just said: "My mother needs me."

They told him that there was no future for him in Lima. That at best he could only be a servant. That he would not be able to help people as he wished. Whereas if he stayed with his uncle he would have comfort, luxury and education. Stubbornly indeed, he stuck to his strange choice: Lima and his mother.

At last they gave up, and Don Juan de Porres said: "I have to go back to Lima for a short time before taking office in

Panama. I will take you back with me. It is also time for you to fulfill your Christian duties. I will see to it that you are confirmed in Lima."

Then Don Juan de Porres turned toward Don Diego de Miranda and, lowering his voice, said: "I will try to put him as an apprentice to Dr. Marcelo de Rivero, a good Lima physician."

And so, for Martín, it was Lima again.

THE THRILL OF LEARNING

Lima. In the cool fog which enshrouded the city at dawn, Martín was running to the Doctor's office. He was now a medical apprentice to Dr. de Rivero. Don Juan de Porres had arranged it all, and then, lighthearted, he had left for Panama. For two years he had been in close contact with Martín at Guayaquil, and yet, from one day to another, he could wholly dismiss his eleven-year-old son from his mind. His own career, that was what mattered to Don Juan de Porres.

Wanted one day, through a whim, pushed away the next as an embarrassing nuisance, at the most just tolerated, these were old familiar experiences to Martín. Such was life. Martín knew. And Lima was still Lima, with insolent wealth and sordid misery. Martín wasted no time in regrets or self pity. He wanted to help people, and he was determined to make the most of this opportunity to study.

Martín roomed with his mother who had moved away from Espíritu Santo Street and lived with another woman. Ana Velásquez was a little awed at this son of hers studying medicine. She was glad that he had come back as he said he would. She was proud of him, and at the same time sad. She knew that no matter how clever Martín was, he could never bring any notable change into her life. He would always be a Negro. There was no escaping that fact. Ever. As far as she was concerned it meant that Don Juan de Porres was, from then on, as good as lost to her.

The Doctor's office, early in the morning, was quiet and mysterious. Rows and rows of bottles, flasks, jars, potteries. Martín swept the floor. He dusted the shelves carefully. Then he changed the water of leeches, shook lightly the cats' skins. At the time both cats' skins and leeches were much in use for medical purposes. Then he sorted out the bundles of freshly gathered herbs and hung them in bunches to dry.

In those days a physician was not only a general practitioner; he was also a chemist and a surgeon. He did everything for people, from cutting their hair to healing their diseases, setting their broken bones and counseling them in their private affairs.

Spanish physicians of the sixteen century were highly regarded the world over. They had been taught by Arabs who, in turn, held their knowledge from the Jews, who themselves had been outstanding physicians from time immemorial.

When the office was in order, Martín went into the garden

and started weeding. The Doctor cultivated all sorts of plants good for ailments. These herbs were used dry in brews to drink, powdered to paste for external use, mixed

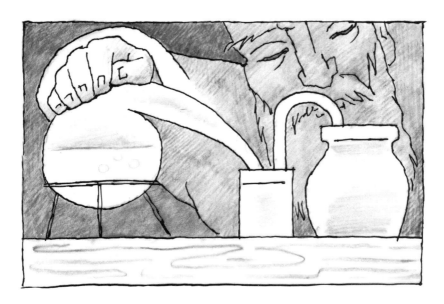

with spirits for remedies. There were so many of them for Martín to learn how to recognize and to memorize the properties thereof: hyssop, camomile, rosemary, rue, mint, cinnamon, arnica, acanthus, borage, sage, cumin, origanum, thyme, balsam, fennel, melissa, etc. Peru itself boasted of many outstanding native healing plants, such as nasturtium, quillái, cinchona, copaiba.

He was glad when the weeding was over. He preferred accompanying the Doctor on outings over the countryside, looking for plants. But more than anything else he loved to go on calls with the Doctor and learn how to examine a sick person, to be able to recognize the disease through the symptoms and make a correct diagnosis, to learn what to prescribe for a particular ailment. On the other hand, during office hours there were always many people with broken bones and ugly wounds to dress, and Martín learned how to do that too.

It was such a busy, hard, but interesting life. And soon Martín decided he would have to live by himself in order to have more time for his home work. He took a small room in the house of a lady by the name of Dona Ventura de Luna. The window of his room opened on a small garden. Martín promptly asked permission to plant a lemon seed. He would be able to watch the plant grow. His very own tree.

In a very short time, his landlady Ventura de Luna was saying, to her neighbors: "I never had a better tenant. He is so clean, so considerate. If it were not that the bell for the first Mass wakes me up every morning I would never hear him leave the house. He is so quiet."

Indeed Martín tiptoed out and ran all the way to the Church of Santo Domingo. Even at that early hour of the day there were plenty of people there. All sorts of people. Rich and poor, men and women, free Negroes and slaves and converted Indians. There, indeed, was no discrimination whatsoever. There was one Church for all, and, at the communion rail, they all knelt together.

Yet Martín was lonely. Juana was in Guayaquil. His father had left him. And his mother did not seem to understand him. But there were his work and his studies. These he loved. He was going to help people, all the unhappy people in Lima, all the unhappy people . . . everywhere. Was he? There were so many of them. There, on his knees, in the Church of Santo Domingo, at dawn, he felt already the burden of other people's woes weighing heavily on his boy's shoulders. It was beyond him, no matter his knowledge, his skill, his willingness, he could not do a full job. The evil was too great. He was helpless. "O God! What shall I do?"

Time went on and Martín advanced in his studies rapidly. Dr. de Rivero was well pleased with him. One day Martín said to Dona de Luna: "Could I have some candles? Of course, not whole ones, just little bits. Some left over."

In the sixteen century there was no other light and candles were so expensive that poor people did not use them. They simply went to bed when it was dark. Ventura de Luna had never thought of leaving any candle with Martín.

"Now what do you suppose he is up to?" she remarked to the neighbors, later. "I'll bet he is going to study all night. You know that he is quite learned: he can read and write even, and he is studying medicine. I shall have to find out what he is going to do with candles. It is not good for a youngster to spend his nights studying."

"Here are some candles, Martín. Tell me, what are you going to do with them?"

Martín flashed his radiant smile: "I just need them. Thank you very much." And he was gone.

Dona Ventura's curiosity left her no peace, especially since Martín seemed to be using the bits of candles very fast. So she got up in the middle of the night and tiptoed toward Martín's room. Sure enough, there was a light showing through the crack under the door. Holding her breath, Dona Ventura put her eye against the keyhole. She suppressed a scream: kneeling by his bed, young Martín was praying, his face covered with tears.

Ventura de Luna decided to say nothing. How could she, anyway, without confessing her curiosity. Besides, what she had seen was not to be taken too seriously. Probably Martín had studied very late and had just started praying when she came. Yet . . . the expression on his face . . . ? Oh well, often boys and girls go through a period of extreme religious fervor in their adolescence before they fall in love. Martín would be like the rest, and would outgrow his religious emotion. Better not mention anything to him. To the neighbors, she just said, raising her hands and lifting up her eyes: "My young roomer, Martín, he is really holy!" And people who could remember Martín's childhood and generosity shook their heads understandingly: "Yes, he was always a good boy, though in a way a little queer at times. Do you remember how he used to give away all his mother's money and food, and go without eating and be beaten into the bargain? A tough youngster. A funny boy. And yet clever. Doctor de Rivero says he is the best medical student he has ever had."

"The Doctor says Martín is born to the job; that he has natural abilities."

"And it is not only that. He has a knack for getting around people. It is not every physician who knows that. It is a great asset to the boy. And he needs it. What with his father gone for good, his poor mother and . . . Too bad . . . too bad . . ."

So ran the gossip. As time went on, poor people who flocked to Dr. de Rivero's office took to liking his young assistant more and more. However, what did disturb them was Martín's extreme youth. Martín himself never gave it a thought. It seemed to him he had been on his own ever since he was born, and anyway, Dr. de Rivero was always there to take the responsibility. However, one particular day, Martín was alone in the office. Dr. de Rivero had had an emergency call. Suddenly shrieks rose in the street, and a moment later someone opened the office door, calling wildly:

"Doctor de Rivero! Come quick! A man has been stabbed to death!"

Martín came out. "Where is the man? Bring him in here," he said.

They did, and as Martín bent over him, the people pushed him aside saying: "Get Dr. de Rivero quick. This is no job for you."

"Dr. de Rivero is on call," said Martín gently, "and I have no way of reaching him. You must let me attend this man at once, or else it will be too late."

"But you are a mere child!" cried a woman. Martín did not answer. Quietly and deliberately, he fetched some water, some clean rags; he chose one of the numerous jars and mixed some white powder in a dish. He bent over the man, an Indian, who was bleeding profusely. Martín washed the wound, put some of the wet powder on it and bandaged the gap deftly. Then he brought out a small bottle, poured some of the liquid in a cup and said to the Indian: "Drink this slowly. You have had a shock. This will do you good." The people now silent, stood watching. As the Indian began to come back to life, Martín said: "Now

you go home and rest. Take the bottle with you and drink what is left. It is wine. It will help you recover. And be sure to come back tomorrow, so that I can put a clean bandage on your wound. You will be all right."

Next day the Indian came back, and how happy was Martín when Dr. de Rivero, after having examined him, said: "Martín, I could not have done any better myself."

Doctor, where is your assistant? He is not sick, is he?"

"Doctor, I have not seen Martín lately. I miss him. Where is he?"

"Doctor, if you don't mind, I would rather have the young chap Martín dress my wound. Can't you get him?"

Doctor de Rivero paused and looked at all the eager faces around him. Then he said gruffly: "Martín has left."

"Left!" The patients gathered anxiously around Dr. de Rivero. An old man asked pointedly: "Got rid of him, Doctor?"

Anger flared within the Doctor as he faced the old man: "So, that's the way you figure it out, is it? Too bad to disappoint you, but I had nothing to do with this. Martín, of his own free will, left me . . . and *you* too."

There was a murmur in the group as the Doctor went on

bitterly: "That's what happens when you befriend a shiftless human being. Years of training, money, care, and when he is ready to repay you, he just picks up and goes leaving you with all the work. And don't think that people are going to be grateful to those like me who stick to their job. Look at you. Where would you be, all of you today, if it were not for me? Now that your darling Martín has left you, where would you be? But you don't care, you still have neither ear nor mouth except for him!"

He stopped, embarrassed at his own outburst. The truth was that the Doctor felt just as bad as the patients did about Martín's departure. Not only was Martín the best student he ever had, but he had liked Martín very much himself.

In the silence that followed, a woman asked softly: "What happened, Doctor?"

The Doctor shrugged his shoulders and said, now in a quiet voice: "Nothing. Nothing that I could foresee anyhow. It all came as a surprise to me. Martín has entered the Dominican convent."

They were speechless and thoughtful. After a while, somebody said: "You know, Doctor, Dominican friars are not cloistered. So Martín could still be a physician and a Dominican monk. I mean he can still make use of what you have taught him, for the good of everybody."

Dr. de Rivero shook his head sadly: "No. Martín has become a servant in the convent."

"A servant!" Now they were crestfallen. Now they were indignant. Now Martín was truly lost to them. They felt abandoned, and in their resentment harsh words came out:

"Trust a pious one to think of himself first!"

"His kindness was only a pretense. He did not really care for us. Or else he would not have left us."

"He is ungrateful. Throwing away all that was bestowed on him."

"He is crazy. He was always slightly cracked, anyhow."

"He just could not stand being alone anymore. So he looked for protection and companionship in a monastery."

"No matter what you say, Negroes cannot make the grade."

"The trouble with Martín was his childhood as an outcast. That childhood was no fault of his own. But he just could not get past those memories."

"Whatever it is, the result is the same. By entering the monastery he betrayed us all. He was one of us, a poor boy. Now, in the monastery he won't have to worry about making a living and he will forget us. He could have helped us all, poor, sick, Negroes, Indians. But he does not care; he is after his own comfort. Or perhaps, after all, he is one of those people so anxious about their own private salvation that the rest of the world can go hang. The whole thing is a disgrace. Such a disappointment! Martín is a traitor."

So they spoke. Meanwhile in the Convent of the Holy Rosary, Martín was sweeping the floor of the cloister. His head was a turmoil and his heart ached. A few days ago it had all come to pass so swiftly. Did he know exactly what he was doing when he knocked at the door of the convent? Did he know what he was going to say? . . . Then, suddenly there was Father Francis de Vega, busy, worried, preoccupied. "What do you want?" "Father, please, is there any

work I can do in the convent?" Father de Vega looked up briefly. He saw a fifteen-year-old healthy Negro in front of him. The convent needed helpers. "How good are you at cutting hair?" he asked casually. That was all. Martín was in. He was given the worn-out habit of a tertiary.

Of course that really meant he was still an outsider. He could go back in the world any time. Now, for instance . . . it was consultation time at Doctor de Rivero's . . . Martín swept more furiously. He did long to be there, helping people as of old. "Well, I *am* going to help them," he kept repeating to himself. "I am." And yet he could not help thinking that it hardly looked as if he had chosen the right way to do so. What he had done did not seem to make sense. And yet he knew, in spite of his heartache, that it was the reason why he had come and sought admission at the convent: in order to help people more completely, in their bodies, in their minds and in their souls.

"Martín! Martín! You had quite a lot to do with sick people, didn't you? Father Pedro de Montesdosca is sick. An infected leg. Go and see if you can cheer him a little. He is in a bad temper and talking of nothing but food. As if someone whose leg is going to be amputated should think of nothing but eating! Go and see what you can do."

Going to have his leg amputated! How dreadful! thought Martín. He knocked at the door of the cell and went in.

"Good morning, Father. What can I do for you?"

Father de Montesdosca had one look at him. "Do for me!" he roared. "You dog of a half-breed! The nerve!"

"Martín is my name," went on Martín evenly. "I have

just started working in the convent, and Father Prior sent me to you . . .''

"Well, go back to the kitchen where you belong. Might make yourself more useful there. I have not had a tasty dish for ages . . . Oh my leg! . . . my leg!''

Martín bowed quietly and went out. A tasty dish? What about a green salad, of varied vegetables . . . with capers . . . ?

Martín was back in the cell. "Father, can you get over your irritation long enough to . . .''

"You again! Get out! Leave me alone!'' And Father Pedro turned his back.

"Please, Father, I know you have all the reasons to feel angry at everybody, but just have a look at this dish I have brought you. It's a salad.''

"A salad?'' asked a muffled voice in the pillow.

"A green salad.''

"A green salad?'' The head moved.

"With capers.''

"With capers! You don't say!'' Father Pedro had turned completely around and was eagerly looking at the plate. "Give me that plate, boy . . . Oh my leg! . . . A caper salad! . . . Oh my leg! . . . The very thing I wanted! How did you guess?''

Martín waited until Father Pedro had finished eating. "And now, Father, may I look at your leg?''

"What's the use? It's an ugly sight. They are going to cut it off anyhow.''

"Just the same . . . If you don't mind?''

Martín washed the leg, applied a remedy and put a clean

bandage around it.

"Well, I must say, it does feel better to get rid of all these dirty rags. Thank you very much, Martín. And for the salad too."

"Eh, there! Martín!" boomed a joyous voice in the cloister the next day. Martín nearly dropped his broom. "Why, Father Pedro! You scared me so! You are up?"

"Up, and on my *two* legs, my boy. Believe it or not, they are not going to amputate. It is much better."

"I am so glad."

"And how do you think *I* feel? I tell you, Martín, you did it. You did!"

"Why, Father, what a tease you are."

"No, I am telling the truth. It was what you did to my leg."

"And the salad of course," chuckled Martín. "Don't forget the salad!" Then he added gently and seriously: "No, Father. *I* did not do it. I nursed you, and God healed you."

It was the classic answer of the old school of physicians, according to the ancient tradition of the father of medicine, Hippocrates, who lived in Greece four centuries before the Christian era. And Martín's answer was true in more than one way.

Clip, clip, clip, went Martín's scissors around the head of Father Santiago. It was a hot day. The Father dozed. Martín tried to remember the convent rules for cutting hair: just a crown around the head, and perfectly even. There, it was finished. He surveyed his work. It looked very neat.

"It's all done, Father."

"Good," said Father Santiago waking up. And he raised his hand and touched his head. "What?" he shrieked. "How dare you? Are you mad? Making me look utterly ridiculous!"

"But, Father, I tried to cut according to the rules."

"Impudent Negro! The rules! Who do you think knows

the rules? You or I? How long have you been here? Are you a Dominican friar? You are nothing but a servant here, and I want you to get through your thick head, once and for all, that my hair is never cut this way. Always, always, I have it longer in front. The curls, right there, on the forehead. The curls! Is that clear? And don't you go around telling me how I should have it, or else I'll have you dismissed in no time."

Weeks went by. Martín kept dreading the time when he would have to cut Father Santiago's hair again. And one day, here was Father Santiago as haughty and determined as ever.

"Now, Martín, no nonsense this time. Remember? Don't you dare touch the front curls!"

"Father," said Martín gently, though his heart was beating fast, "Father, you called me a servant. And right you are. I am serving in the Dominican Order. Therefore I must obey the rule of the Dominican Order. So what else can I do but cut your hair according to the Dominican rule?"

"I shall report you!" bellowed Father Santiago, sweeping out of the room in a rage.

Oh, dear, how complicated life was, even in a priory. A trifle, like the cutting of a hair! Martín sighed. Was he right to have stood his ground? Was it not much easier to just agree? Why make such a fuss? Who cared? But was he not the barber of the convent? Had not Father Prior told him the rules for cutting?

He was still brooding when the crowd of novices came in to have their own hair cut. Martín liked the novices very much. They were young. Several of them not older than he was. They were gay, mischievous and friendly. They came in giggling more than they usually did.

"Hey, Martín. Do you know the latest?"

He shook his head.

"Well, don't faint when we tell you. Martín, you are making history in the dignified Convent of the Holy Rosary."

"What's the joke?" asked Martín, who could not help smiling at them.

"No joke," they said. "The truth, the naked truth. We have just heard. From now on, it is the *regular* Dominican haircut for everybody. *Everybody*. Do you get it? 'You-know-who,' was he mad! But Father Prior's orders are strict: *everybody*. Good work, Martín."

Martín bent and picked up an imaginary something from the floor to hide his embarrassment and also his satisfaction. Then he said lightly: "Let's get on with your hair, all of you."

Clip, clip, clip. They sat around watching him, talking to each other, discussing a point of their study, and often referring it to Martín. "What do you think, Martín?" They knew he was really telling them his own thoughts, not what he had been taught. They felt free and confident with him. He was their age, he understood and yet somehow he seemed to have such wisdom. They loved the hair-cutting period with Martín.

Then they began to poke fun at each other. And finally, the teasing centered on one of them, Cypriano. Cypriano came from a well-to-do Spanish family in Peru, but his looks were against him. He was small for his age, and so covered with hair that his comrades could not help cracking jokes about him: "Look at him? Eh, monkey! He forgot to grow. He likes best to swing from a tree!" and so on. Cypriano was good-natured. He usually laughed with them, and that day he did too. However, the novices kept at it so long that he grew silent, his back hunched and his mouth set.

Clip, clip, clip . . . and the roar of laughter from the teasers. And, suddenly, Martín's quiet, low and firm voice:

"Little Brother Cypriano has still time to grow. And he will. He will be a man of finer physique than any of you. And he will rise to such a position that he will leave every single one of you far below."

They were thunderstruck, not only at the prediction but at the sureness with which it was voiced. They looked at Martín in awe. He had completely sobered them and they felt ashamed of themselves.

As to Cypriano, later in life, when he had become a fine-looking man and had been made a bishop, he liked to retell that episode, and how Martín's words had saved him at the time from giving up his religious vocation and also from losing confidence in himself altogether.

Thus, in the convent, already Martín was giving to others the benefit of his talent as physician of the body, the mind and the soul. Yet his unusual ability in these matters was not really recognized at the time. It is true that beside cutting hair he had been assigned to the infirmary and the care of the sick. But there were many other duties taking up his time which were hardly in keeping with the medical profession, such as taking care of the entire wardrobe of the monks, scrubbing floors and cultivating the vegetables and herb garden.

To all this was added another duty: scavenging. In those days in Lima, garbage was taken care of by the wild blue-neck turkey buzzards, the gallinazos, but, of course they did not take care of the toilets. Somebody had to do that. And in the convent, this duty was assigned to Martín.

"Well, Martín, how do you like it?" asked one of the monks jovially. "Would not you be better off in the palace of the Archbishop of Mexico than here cleaning toilets?"

The Archbishop of Mexico? Martín had nothing against him. For all he knew the Archbishop might be a saintly man. But, about a palace, Martín knew only too well, and what it usually does to people who live in it. Luxury and honors separate us from God and from our fellow men.

Brush in hand and a twinkle in his eyes, Martín straightened up and said: "I had rather be a doorkeeper in the house of my God than to dwell in the tents of wickedness."

"Why, Martín!" gasped the monk. "Where did you learn that?"

"It's in the Eighty-Fourth Psalm, Father."

"Right, right. Well . . . well . . . well. . . . Of course, you understand, I was only joking. I meant that, after all, you do not have to do that work. You are not bound by any vow. You can leave the convent. You could even set up a medical practice of your own in town. You are young and healthy. You could find yourself a wife. You don't have to accept this life here. You are free. Think it over. What are you after? What do you seek?"

Yes, what? Was he staying just because he feared being alone in the world? Was he after shelter, protection, companionship, his own private salvation? Or was he above all, following his feeling that by serving God first he would end by serving people best.

YEARS WENT BY, and one day, in the land of Panama, the Governor, Don Juan de Porres, heard that Martín, his son, had entered the Dominican convent. At first Don Juan de Porres was pleased: Martín in a convent, that was very appropriate, very dignified and it relieved his father of any sense of responsibility which occasionally (oh, very occasionally) might prey on his mind.

But Don Juan de Porres's satisfaction did not last when he heard that Martín had not taken any vows and was doing menial work. Menial work! A de Porres! What a disgrace! The pride of the grandee of Spain was hurt. He was not going to let matters stand that way. There must be a mistake somewhere. Perhaps the Provincial did not know who Martín was. Don Juan de Porres would see to it that he was told and that Martín would be made a priest which was the only proper position for a de Porres in a priory.

So, in due time, Father Prior of the Dominican Convent of the Holy Rosary called Martín:

"Martín, we have heard from your father. It is his wish that you enter Holy Orders, and become a Dominican of the First Order."

"Oh, no!" cried Martín impulsively. "Oh, no! I could not possibly. Honest, I could not."

The Prior was embarrassed.

"Well, at least, you could be made a regular lay brother and take the vows."

By then Martín, usually so self-composed, was in tears and he begged to be left as he was.

The Prior did not quite know what to make of this. He wanted to please Don Juan de Porres, but on the other hand, Martín was most useful to the convent just as a helper, and since at least for the time being, Martín himself did not care for a change . . . Well, anyhow, the Prior could not be blamed for not having tried to do what Don Juan de Porres wanted. And Panama was far away. . . . So the Prior did not insist any further.

It was the third time within the twenty years of his life that Martín had made a strange choice. The two other times were when he had chosen to come back to Lima instead of remaining comfortably at Guayaquil, and when he had chosen to leave Dr. de Rivero. And each time, people talked and wondered and disapproved and branded him a coward or one of a diseased mind, or a victim of childhood circumstances. Everybody had his own opinion regarding Martín's choices, and still has today for that matter.

Martín's life went on as usual after the Prior had made the offer of priesthood or lay brotherhood. Still the same duties, and plenty of work. However, from time to time more and more strange reports reached the Prior. There was for instance the mouse story:

Mice were everywhere in the convent, and a religious had set a trap. A mouse was caught, but Martín, discovering this, had set the mouse free, though it was a notorious fact that the convent was infested with these destructive animals.

Later, while Martín was hoeing in the garden, the sacristan monk came over to him carrying a bundle under his arm:

"Well, I suppose, Martín, you are pleased with yourself. You think you are a great help to the convent raising vegetables, don't you? Meanwhile, through the great kindness of your heart, there won't be any altar cloths left presently. Look."

And the sacristan threw his bundle of linen at Martín's feet. The altar cloths were full of mice holes.

"What do you mean?" queried Martín.

"Just look at your work, my friend. Your work. The work of your tender, oh, ever so tender feeling . . . for mice. You could not stand a mouse in a trap. Oh, no! You'd rather have us all go begging. But I tell you, I have had enough, and so has the Prior. And whether you like it or not, the orders are strict now. You are to set traps everywhere, and *kill* the pests."

"But," cried Martín, "mice mean no harm. They are just hungry."

"Just hungry! Just hungry! Hear him! And what about us? Us? Are you stupid, or trying to be smart?

Take your choice: it is the mice or the convent."

"And then, Father Prior," said the sacristan as he related the story, "I walked away from the garden. But before I was out I heard a low sound. I turned around, and saw Martín standing there, whistling. I hid behind a bush. And presently I saw a mouse scurrying through the garden toward Martín. And then two, three, six, twelve, and dozens and dozens of them. What a sight! They all raced toward Martín, and in no time at all there was a crowd of them around him. Then Martín sat down on his heels, and I heard him say: "Little brothers and sisters, please follow me. You cannot stay in the convent any more. You will have to go and live in the barn. If you do, I promise I will go and feed you every day." Then he got up and went toward the barn. And believe it or not, Father Prior, all the mice followed him. They did, Father Prior, they did! I saw them with my own eyes."

"When did this happen?" inquired Father Prior.

"A week ago."

"And since then?"

"There are no mice in the convent whatsoever. They are all in the barn, and Martín feeds them. Everyday. From kitchen scraps."

Father Prior was silent. Perhaps he recalled another young man, Francis of Assisi, who three hundred years before, in Italy, also had talked to animals and made them follow his gentle way.

But Father Prior had more to contend with than mice. The convent was deep in debt. Father Prior decided to sell a

valuable painting. He tucked it under his arm and walked out through the garden where Martín was hoeing. Martín wondered as he saw him go. A moment later a religious came by and asked Martín if he had seen Father Prior. Martín told him Father Prior had gone out carrying a framed painting under his arm. "Ah, yes," said the monk, "I guess it has come to that. He has to sell it. We need money so badly."

Martín threw his hoe down and ran out full speed into the street, looking up and down for Father Prior. Ah, there he was, and Martín all out of breath caught up with him.

"Father Prior! Father Prior! Don't sell the picture. Look at me. I am strong and healthy. I will go in bondage until the convent's debts are paid."

Father Prior was stunned. What was this? How could Martín make such an offer? What kind of generosity was this? Everybody would call it wrong, or simply mad. But Father Prior set the picture down against the wall of a house. He put his two hands on Martín's shoulders, and looking straight into the clear and kind eyes of the young man he said:

"My son, you are indeed a true disciple of the One who gave up everything for the sake of mankind. And your place is among us Dominicans who try to follow Him. You do belong to the great Dominican family. I know of your reluctance to accept Holy Orders, and I shall respect your wish. But lay brotherhood is different. Go back to the convent, Martín. You will be received as a lay brother. And this time, there is no saying no. It is a command."

In the Chapter Hall of the convent, all are assembled. The Dominican monks in their white flowing wool robes and black long capes, the lay brothers with their white habit covered in front and back with black pieces of cloth called scapulars, and the novices with the white habits and the short black mantles.

Martín approaches the altar. He prostrates himself on the floor, face down, resting on his folded arms.

In a powerful voice, the Prior asks: *"Quid quaeris?"* What do you seek?

And Martín answers the traditional words: *"Misericordia Dei et vestram."* God's mercy and yours.

Ah, yes, indeed, that is what he had been seeking, ever since he was a little boy. How else, except through God's mercy, could he ever meet the passionate concern of his heart? He had to be wholly consecrated to God in order to be wholly free to help mankind. Only through God could he serve people best.

The Prior explains that when one becomes a religious it is not enough just to be good. That one has to be voluntarily poor, voluntarily obedient, voluntarily pure. And he asks: "Are you willing?"

And Martín answers: *"Volo."* I am.

Then a white new habit is brought, and a black scapular, and a belt which is called a cord. All kneel and sing the old hymn attributed to Charlemagne, *"Veni Creator Spiritus,"* Come Holy Spirit, Creator come. Martín is raised up, and is given the habit, the scapular and the cord, and all sing the *"Te Deum,"* All praise to Thee, O God.

And so did Martín de Porres become a lay Dominican brother, at the age of twenty-four, in 1603, in Lima, Peru.

HOPELESS MARTIN

Under the arcades of the Plaza de Armas, a young handsome Indian sat next to the public writer. From time to time he drew a few notes from his hand-made Pan-pipe of llama bones, beautifully decorated.

"It's nice," said the public writer. "Will you teach me how to play?"

"If you wish," said the young Indian. "That's about the only thing left for us Indians to do — to teach music. Would you like to learn on a wooden flute? Or what about starting on one of our whistles shaped like animals, a monkey, a dog, a bird?"

"No," said the writer, "I would prefer to learn on a Panpipe like yours."

"It is difficult," said the Indian. "It will take a long time."

"I can pay you back by teaching you how to write."

"I don't care about writing. That is not necessary. No one in the Inca Empire ever knew about writing. Not even the Inca himself, the King."

"I know," said the writer, "that you Indians of Peru never had any written signs whatsoever. But now that we Spaniards are here, you need to know about writing. Everybody has to write a letter, some time or another."

"I don't worry about that. When I need something in writing, I don't have to pay for it. I know a chap who does it for me."

"Who? A professional public writer like me?"

"No. Martín. At the Dominican convent. You know, the young man who used to be Dr. de Rivero's assistant."

"Ah, yes, I have heard about him. A métis, isn't he? And a little strange too. But, I guess, doing much good. I bet he is going to make a convert out of you."

The young Indian's face darkened. He said nothing, picked up his Panpipe and played softly for quite a time. Then he stopped, licked his lips, wiped his mouth. His expression was serene again as he spoke slowly.

"I go to Martín precisely because he does not try to convert me. With all the others I feel that when they are nice to me it is because they want to prove to me that their God is all right, or because they want to be pleased with themselves, or else because they want to rope me into their church. But with Martín there is no catch. It is straight from the heart. When he gives me something I don't even feel I am receiving anything. I feel as if *I* were the one who gives him something."

"That's quite a trick," laughed the public writer. "Your Martín is a bit of a magician, I guess."

"If you wish. But we, the poor, the Indians, the Negroes, the sick, the abandoned, we just trust him, though at first, when he entered the convent, we were disappointed."

"Why?"

"Well, you see, when he was Dr. de Rivero's assistant he was a friend to all of us. He was one of us. Just as he had been ever since he was a little child. Then he went to the convent, and we felt he had deserted us. As if he had gone on the other side of the fence you might say. Some among us were so bitter that they called him a traitor. But now they don't; nobody does."

"What made them change their mind?"

"Well, it is plain that Martín is no different from what he was. He is even more of a friend to us than ever before. For instance, with him, everything that is good belongs to everybody who needs it."

"What do you mean?"

"Just that. Anything, like food and clothing and shelter, and care in sickness, it's for everybody who needs it, to be had freely, like sunshine and wind."

"You are a poet," said the public writer, "and your Martín sounds like one too. It's all very nice, but, my dear young friend, somebody has to pay nevertheless for all that food, clothing and shelter and medical care."

"Nobody ought to," said the young Indian thoughtfully. "Nobody did in our Empire."

"Well, it's because you were not civilized."

"Ah? Then, to be civilized is when the poor have to pay for food and clothing and shelter and medicine? But how can they, since they are poor? It does not make sense."

"You are the one without any sense, I mean civilized sense," said the Spaniard somewhat contemptuously. "Don't expect me to explain to you our way of life. You would not understand, you don't even know how to write."

"Do all Spanish people know how to write?" inquired the Indian.

"Of course not! Or else I would be out a job!" said the Spaniard impatiently.

"Then one may be civilized without knowing how to write?"

"Oh dear!" wailed the public writer. "You are obstinate. I just wanted to explain to you that you and your Martín are dreamers. You spoke about food, clothing, shelter and medicine as 'free as the sunshine and the wind,' to use your own words. Well, my point is that even if you seem to get it free through Martín, yet don't fool yourself. Somebody has to pay for it. And in this case, it is the Dominican convent, no doubt. I wonder how the monks like it . . ."

Indeed at that very moment Martín was facing Father Prior, who was scolding him severely.

"It is most commendable to be so concerned with the poor,

the sick and the abandoned, Martín. But there is a limit to what the convent can do. You cannot take in everybody as you have been doing, until all cells, empty rooms and even the halls are crowded with unfortunate people. It makes no sense at all. The Dominican convent cannot look after all the needy people in Lima, Martín. We cannot do it, and, don't imagine that you can either. You are not going to get rid of all the evil on this earth just by yourself. It is fool-hardy and presumptuous to think so. Anyway, you have already more than you can do medically speaking just in taking care of the three hundred religious in the convent, without even mentioning your other duties. Therefore, from now on, I expressly forbid you to take in any outsider."

Martín went away heavyhearted.

He was glad that this was the day for him to go to the convent farm, Limatambo. Working in the fields would do him good.

He walked on the country road, and soon his sadness melted away. Lima's surrounding country was covered with orchards, and, because of the mildness of the climate and the excellent system of irrigation which the Spaniards had learned from the Indians, crop after crop succeeded each other the year around.

As he passed a fig orchard, Martín heard the noise of crack-ing branches and saw spots of color in a tree. He went toward it and discovered some ragged children hidden up in the tree.

"What are you doing up there?"

"Nothing," said the boy.

"We have never any figs at our house," said the girl.

"We cannot afford them, they cost too much."

Martín knew what that meant. He remembered.

"Come down," he ordered.

They did, looking very scared. In Lima, stealing fruit from the orchards meant jail for children. Martín sat down by the roadside and motioned for them to sit too, on either side of him. He was very quiet, for what seemed to the children a long time. They did not dare disturb him. His eyes were closed. Perhaps he was praying. When he opened them at last he said quietly:

"Would you like to have your own fig orchard, your very own, where you could go and eat freely whenever you wanted to?"

They looked at him with questioning eyes. He had not scolded them. He had said nothing about jail. Evidently he was all right. But to ask if they would like to have their own orchard? He must be a little bit out of his mind.

"You got loads of money?" inquired the boy cautiously.

Martín shook his head.

"Can you perform miracles?" asked the girl somewhat hopefully.

Martín shook his head.

"Then," said the boy, "about the orchard of our own, that's just a nice story, eh?"

Martín put his hands in his big Dominican sleeves and brought out two figs. "Oh," they shrieked, "where did you get them?"

He laughed happily. "That's the beginning of the orchard," he said. "Now, no more stealing, understand?

You come and see me at Limatambo, the day after tomorrow."

"Why?"

"About your orchard."

As soon as Martín arrived at Limatambo he paid a visit to the horses and the mules. With incredible speed he washed and brushed them, put clean hay in their stables and brought them feed, all the while talking to them. Whenever Martín came to Limatambo it was like a holiday for the animals, and they knew it. They always welcomed him noisily, whinnying, stamping their feet and flinging their tails. Their care was an extra chore that Martín voluntarily took upon himself.

He was supposed to plant some new fig trees. As soon as he was through with the animals he set to work, carefully preparing the soil and handling each sapling with respect and love, and offering it to God and the Blessed Virgin, before planting it in the ground. He seemed to go at it slowly, but it was only because his gestures were rhythmical like a dance. As a matter of fact he was working very fast, because he wanted to have some extra time left.

While he was at Limatambo, he inquired if there was any piece of land around which had not been claimed; that is, which did not belong to anybody. There was. He went to see it. When he came back he worked faster than ever, and on the third day, in the morning, he had finished with his planting. So he set aside all the saplings that were left over, and as he did so, the two children arrived.

They were not alone. They had brought with them several of their friends, poor children of Lima slums. Point-

ing to them, the two children said to Martín: "They want
an orchard too!"

"Fine! Fine!" exclaimed Martín. "That's just the spirit.
Now, you girls, take all the saplings. And you boys, here
are the spades. And now, let us go."

"Where to?" they inquired.

"To your orchard!"

Ah! What a day of happiness this was! Martín and the
boys and girls planting the little trees on the unclaimed piece
of land. Their orchard, the orchard of the poor children in
Lima, for years to come.

Many such an orchard did Martín plant in his lifetime:
fig, olive and orange orchards which became the common
property of the poor of Lima. Martín showed the people,
children and adults, how to cultivate and harvest. In this
way, many children whose parents could not afford a private

orchard had plenty of fruit. Some of the olive orchards are still there now, though the trees had to be replaced through the centuries. Yet they were originally planted by Martín.

On his way back to the convent he hurried for fear of being late. It was getting dark. He turned into the convent street. Who was there, propped against the wall of the convent? An old man. "Eh, Grandpa," said Martín, "you'd better go home." No answer. The man did not move. Martín bent down. The old man was covered with sores and his eyes were closed. Quickly, Martín put his head against the man's chest: his heart was still beating, but very faintly. It was evident that the man would be incapable of standing on his feet. Martín looked up and down the street. Nobody. What could he do? He could not leave the old man there with the night coming on. The man would be dead in the morning. One more look in the deserted street, then Martín lifted the frail body, set it on his shoulder and made for the convent kitchen door. He was lucky; no one was there. Hurrying on tiptoes through the halls with his burden, he reached his cell, closed the door, laid the old man on his bed, and breathed a sigh of relief: nobody had seen him.

Martín revived the old man, washed him and took care of his sores. Then he left him to go to evening prayers. Afterwards he went to the kitchen and gathered what everybody thought was his own meal and went back to his cell.

For several days Martín kept the old man in his cell, taking care of him. He himself slept on the floor and gave his

patient most of his own food. After a while the old man
began to recover, and by and by he felt strong enough to
leave the convent.

"Good," said Martín. "Now, just sit down a minute.
I will get something in the kitchen for you to take with you
on your way. Just wait. I'll be right back."

He was. "There!" he said triumphantly as he opened his
cell door, carrying some cooked yuccas in his hand. But his
smile froze on his face: near the old man stood a lay brother
looking as dark as a cloud.

"Good morning, Brother," said Martín in an effort to be
natural. Then he went to the old man, gave him the yuccas
and said gently: "And now, you better be on your way,
Grandpa."

The old man was gone, but the lay brother was still there.
Martín hoped that the brother did not know how many days
the man had been in his cell. Nor that he was so sick.
Martín had covered up the bed before going to the kitchen.
Perhaps the brother thought the man had just come in. Even
that was bad enough after the Prior had forbidden Martín to
bring any outsider into the cells.

The lay brother did not say a word. He just marched
toward the bed and threw back the covers. "Look at it!
Look at it!" he bellowed. "It's an outrage! An outrage!
You are hopeless, Martín. Hopeless. Look at those blankets! The convent's blankets! All stained with blood and
pus. I shall complain."

"Please don't, Brother," said Martín hastily, joining his
hands in supplication. "Listen to me. Blankets, I can wash.

Soap and water will remove the stains. But it would take more than soap and water to clean a soul who failed to help a neighbor in need."

"If you had any sense at all just now," shrieked the brother, red with anger, "you would have apologized for your foul deed, or at least kept your mouth shut, instead of insulting me."

"What?" cried Martín. "But, Brother, I was only thinking of my . . ."

But the lay brother was gone, straight to the Prior.

Once more Martín was reprimanded, and this time given a severe penance for his disobedience. When he had accomplished it he went back to report to the Prior.

"You have to understand, Martín, as a lay brother you have to obey orders from your superiors. Is that clear?"

"Not quite, Father," said Martín humbly.

"Well, what is it?"

"Reverend Father, I thank you for being so patient with me. Please do set me straight, for I am greatly puzzled. Was it really wrong to put charity before obedience?"

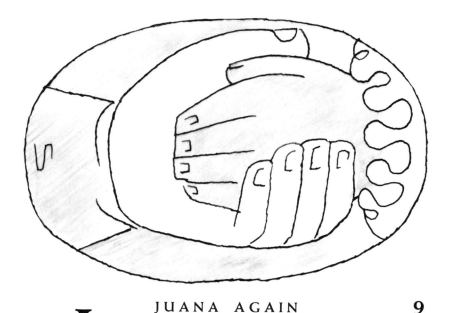

J UANA RETURNED from Guayaquil, an accomplished, lovely girl. Martín was overjoyed. She was engaged to a man Martín liked very much, and she even had the proper dowry necessary for her marriage.

In those days, in Peru, no girl could marry without a dowry, neither could she become a nun without it. So, for those who did not have any money there was nothing left to do except to become servants or beggars.

The date for the wedding was set. Juana was very excited. She said to Martín: "I worry about the money of the dowry; all these gold pieces, in a small bag at home. Suppose they are stolen. It would be horrible. Martín, won't you please do me a favor? Take them to the convent and keep them there until the wedding day. In the convent they will be perfectly safe."

Martín took the bag and hid it in his cell. He felt very happy thinking of Juana, and next day there was a song in his heart as he made his way to the kitchen. There, as usual, all his "friends" were waiting for him, poor people who never knew a square meal. Martín always found enough leftovers in the convent kitchen to feed them. Somehow, under Martín's hands there always seemed to be enough food to go around.

But that morning, it was more than a question of food. As he entered the kitchen he was confronted with a crowd of people, men, women and children who had nothing on but pieces of rags. They had bartered everything the day before, they said, in order to eat. Martín was crestfallen. He could manage to feed them, but clothe them he could not. He knew it was out of the question to ask the Prior. It was already too good of him to close his eyes on Martín's daily distribution of food in the convent. Yet, clothes these people must have, and right away.

Then, suddenly, Martín remembered. That money, in his cell! Enough to clothe the whole crowd.

"Wait!" he said briskly, and disappeared. In a moment he was back, carrying the small bag full of gold pieces. "Come with me," he said. They all hurried out after him. He took them to a merchant and clothed them all.

When he came back to the convent the bag was empty. Juana's dowry money was gone. Only then did Martín begin to realize what he had done. And, as of old, he poured his heart out to God: Today those people were naked. Today I had the money. Juana does not need money today.

But those people did, right away. So today the money was for them. When Juana needs it next week, she should have it too. God, help me to find it.

But the days passed and no money. Such a large sum could not easily be gathered. Martín prayed a great deal and thought of many ways. And, of course, Juana knew nothing about all this. She was very busy with the wedding preparation.

The day before the wedding Martín went out for some errand. He was tired: he had prayed all night long. As he went by the shop of a chemist, Don Mateo Pastor, who had been a good friend of his ever since he was a student at Dr. de Rivero's, he felt like stopping for a few minutes. He went in, and no sooner had he greeted Don Pastor that he found himself telling him the whole story of Juana's dowry and the naked people.

"Reckless Martín!" said Don Pastor, gravely shaking his head. "You had no business doing such a thing. You were wrong. That money was entrusted to you. It was not your money. It was Juana's money. You had no right to dispose of it."

"You mean," asked Martín, "that I should have let those people die of cold, though that day I happened to have the money right there to prevent it?"

"You always have a good answer," said Don Pastor a little sharply. "However, you must realize, Martín, that some people may take advantage of the kindness of your heart. How do you know that it was not a put-up job, those naked people? Just a way of getting clothes free?"

"Is it not better to be taken advantage of ten times rather than leave one human being in real want once?" queried Martin.

"Another good answer, eh? You are smart, my friend. Meanwhile, there is Juana."

"Yes, there is Juana," sighed Martín bending his head.

"I think I had better call my wife on this," said Don Pastor. "Francisca!"

Francisca came in. She listened to the tale. She was horrified: "Oh poor, poor Juana! Martín, how could you?"

He did not say anything. As of old he was torn by the same question: the family or the stranger in need, Juana or the naked people? O Lord, I don't know. It is too difficult.

Finally Francisca turned to her husband: "We cannot let this happen, can we, Mateo? The wedding is to be tomorrow. There is no time to lose."

And so it came to pass that next day Don Pastor accompanied Martín to the wedding ceremony, and he handed him a full purse just at the moment Martín was supposed to give Juana's dowry to the bridegroom. And so, after all, Juana was happily married.

Martín was full of thanksgiving to God who had so inspired Don Pastor and his wife and he went to thank them both.

"Don't mention it," said Don Pastor. "We are glad we could do it. All is well that ends well. But don't do it again, Martín!"

Martín smiled happily. Then he said, "You know, never before did I realize the terrible plight of girls in Lima who have no money. Not all of them are so lucky as Juana.

What is to become of them?"

"Ah, yes," said Francisca, "that's why so many of them turn out badly."

"Something ought to be done," said Martín thoughtfully.

"Well now," said Don Mateo Pastor laughing, "don't tell me, Martín, that you have already another plan up your sleeve! Out with it my friend. What's on your mind?"

The upshot of all this was that Don Pastor and his wife pledged themselves to contributing dowries for twenty-seven penniless girls. This was the beginning of a dowry fund for the marriage of poor girls in Lima. Martín called on many wealthy conquistadors to join the fund. He had a way of asking which was quite irresistible. He was gentle and at the same time very forceful, so sure was he that he was right. He made everybody feel that this was not alms, but an obligation of the whole community to take care of the girls. And, in that way, the girls themselves did not feel embarrassed at accepting the money.

After the Prior had expressly forbidden him to fill the convent with sick and abandoned people, Martín sent them to his mother and went there to give them medical care daily. Thus he established the first free clinic in the New World. Ana Velásquez put up with it for a long time until Martín began to bring also stray dogs. She complained bitterly to Martín that the dogs dirtied her house. Juana happened to be there when this took place, and later she told her husband:

"Mother was quite beyond herself. It is true that she has been patient with Martín's clinic for poor people. But the animals, that was too much. Well, you should have seen Martín! He called all the dogs and said to them: 'Now, what is the matter with you? You are being taken care of, you have a nice home, and that is the way you thank the kind lady — dirtying her house! Shame on you! From now on everything you have to do, you do outside.' Whereupon all the dogs went out, heads down and tails between their legs!"

And Juana laughed. Then she added seriously: "Mother is getting old. I guess we shall have to take care of Martín's friends, both people and animals."

"Too bad he did not think of making the animals behave while they were still in the convent," remarked her husband.

Juana laughed again gaily. "Oh," she said, "in the convent, there were other causes of trouble. For instance the story about the procurator's dog. That did not help Martín's four-legged friends."

"What was that?"

"Well, the procurator had a dog. For eighteen years. Of course the poor animal was old and not of any use anymore. So the procurator decided to ask somebody to take him away and leave him in a faraway place. This was done. Several times. Each time the dog managed to drag himself back to his master. Anybody's heart would have been moved. But not the procurator's, and he gave orders to have the dog killed. Martín met the people who were carrying the dog to place him where the gallinazos would come and eat it. On hearing the story Martín was indignant. He took the dog away, brought him to his cell, and, somehow, nursed him back to life. The dog, of course started to follow him everywhere, and in the kitchen Martín was overheard telling

him: 'Now, don't you ever go back to your ungrateful
master. You must know by this time how little your long
years of faithfulness have been appreciated.' And so the
procurator came to know that his dog was still alive. He
called Martín. No sooner was Martín in his presence than
he said reproachfully to the procurator: 'Father, why did
you give orders to do away with that dog? Is that the kind
of reward you think his years of faithfulness deserve?'"

"What did the procurator say?"

"I don't know, but I think Martín was right. From the
time he was a little boy, I can remember how he always
treated animals as if they were people, with kindness and
courtesy. He called them creatures of God. All animals
like him. He told me that in the convent barn, he has a dog,

a cat and her kittens and a mouse, all eating out of the same dish."

"No?"

"Oh yes! And he talks to birds too. He even has a hawk who pays him regular visits. The hawk is grateful because one day he fell in the convent garden, after he had been wounded in the leg by a hunter. He had managed to fly away, but he was exhausted. Martín went to him and looked at his leg. He made a splint and bandaged it and . . ."

"Oh, come, come, Juana! Do you know that a hawk is a ferocious and powerful bird, and you would have me believe that Martín bandaged its leg!"

"He did! He did!" insisted Juana stamping her foot. "Martín did. And the hawk was cured. And he flew away. But he comes back every so often . . ."

". . . to eat the birds in the convent garden," interrupted her husband teasingly.

"You are impossible," wailed Juana. "You don't know Martín. When Martín is around nobody eats anybody else. The hawk just pays a friendly visit. He perches on Martín's shoulder, and . . . kisses him."

"Brrr! The kiss of a hawk! Now, Juana, I bet you just added that to the story, that touch, about the kiss."

Juana reddened and flung defiantly: "Well, suppose I did, is that more extraordinary than what happened the other day when Martín stopped the enraged bull in the middle of the street? Nobody could approach the foaming animal. And Martín went up to him with his hands extended, talked to him and quieted him completely. You know this just as well as I do."

"That is true," acknowledged her husband. "I have heard it said also that Martín has a way with flowers and plants. Everything he tends grows beautifully. No doubt, there is a lot to your brother Martín. And I guess we should do everything we can to help him."

They did. And it was a cause of sorrow and concern to Martín when, a few years later, Juana's husband passed away, leaving her with a young girl, Catalina, and but very scant financial means.

Martín was very fond of his niece Catalina. Catalina loved dancing and beautiful clothes which, of course, her mother could not afford. One day, Martín found Catalina in tears. There was going to be a festival in Lima and she had no party coat. Martín did not say anything, but next day there came a young Negro to Juana's door, with six coats on his arm. He said that Brother Martín had sent him, so that Catalina could choose the coat she liked best.

Such was Martín's way, and what he did for Catalina he did for other people. "It is not because they are poor that they should not choose," he used to say. "When they need something give them several to choose from." Of course many people criticized him and found his way extravagant. "Why," they said, "the idea! Poor people should be grateful to be given anything at all. Martín is spoiling them, making them fussy, which they have no right to be."

But to Martín they had the right that any human being has, as a child of God, of being treated as an equal. Martín understood charity in the full meaning of the Hebrew word in the Holy Scriptures, which is compassion and justice.

Juana remarried, Augustán Galán de la Magdalena, and

from then on she was in better circumstances. However, for a long time she remained fearful of being in want. So much so that she became very worried, and secretly had a false key made to fit the desk where her husband kept her money. The false key was brought to her one evening and she hid it, having said nothing about it to anyone.

At that time Juana did not live far from Martín's convent, and every morning she used to be wakened by the bell of the convent which Martín was ringing. The morning after she had received the false key, she woke up at the same time by force of habit, but did not hear any bell. Knowing how punctual Martín was, she thought: He must be sick, and she got up, dressed in haste and hurried to the convent. In the street she saw Martín coming toward her, and as he approached, his face looked severe. As soon as he reached her he said, "How could you, Juana? How could you have done such a wicked thing? To have a false key made to rob your husband."

Juana gasped. How did Martín know? And, besides, she had never thought of this as stealing. But Martín was adamant: "Throw away that key," he said sternly, "and forget about the desk. Am I not here to help you in all your needs?"

Juana went home, threw away the key and never again did she let herself become so worried about money.

Nevertheless she retained her quick temper. One day she, her husband, Catalina and some friends they had invited went to their country house. Somehow it happened that Juana and her husband quarreled on the way and did not stop after they had arrived at their country house. Finally it turned out to be such a bitter quarrel that none of the guests felt like staying, and everybody went out to harness the mules to go back to the city.

Precisely at that time, Martín appeared, staff in hand, his large hat hanging over his shoulder, carrying a basket.

"Here I am!" he called gaily. "I have come to join the party. Now, do not quarrel anymore, I know all that has happened."

How could he? He had not talked to anyone yet. But he set his basket down and started explaining: "Now, Juana . . . Now Augustán . . ." And he unraveled the whole problem and showed them where they had been right and wrong. As they listened to him they quieted down and finally seeing how foolish they had been they apologized to each other. Whereupon Martín joyously lifted the lid of his basket and brought out luscious pies, spiral loaves of bread, grapes and wine. The friends hurried to unharness the mules again, and everybody sat around for a gay picnic.

Martín's reputation for patching up quarrels between husbands and wives spread far and wide, and he became the counselor and adviser of many people; poor, rich, Indians, Negroes, and even important Spaniards such as the Doctor in Laws Don Baltasar Carasco de Horasco, who had such confidence in him that one day he said to Martín:

"Please, call me 'son.' "

"Now," said Martín, "how could this be? I, your father? It would not look well for you."

"Not at all," replied Don Baltasar Carasco de Horasco. "Everybody knows that I am a Spaniard. But, of course," he added with a twinkle in his eye, "it might not look well for

you. They might say that *you* have a Spaniard for a son!"

They both laughed heartily, and Martín said. "All right, all right, *son*. Then your children will be my grandchildren."

So, gradually, Martín was making a host of friends. He was outspoken, firm and yet full of understanding. He did not lack a sense of humor either. One day, a very stern religious criticized another religious for looking too elegant.

"Oh well," said Martín smoothly, "did you ever stop to think whether your own looks might always inspire people to draw nearer to God? Your careless way of dressing, just as if you had thrown your habit over you, your shoes as big as boats, your frowning brow, all that might scare to death a worldly person. Whereas our elegant brother will win him over by the very giddiness of his looks. There are many ways in God."

So he said, out of his own thinking and experience. But it appears that he was also able to quote in Latin appropriately, not only from the Bible, but also from the Fathers of the Church, and so he could help novices through intricate theological and philosophical questions.

There were indeed no walks of life where Martín's help did not prove efficient and beneficent not only to individuals but to the whole community of Lima.

JUVENILE DELINQUENCY ran high in Lima. Neglected or abandoned children of all races roamed the streets. They formed gangs which stole, looted and destroyed and finally ended up behind prison bars.

The new and daring ventures of Martín — the common orchards, the dowries, the clinic — were not enough. Something had to be done specially for the young gangsters. At least Martín thought so. He went to see the Prior.

"Yes," said the Prior, "they are a bad lot, those young ones. Budding criminals, that's what they are."

"But they don't have to be," said Martín. "If they were given proper food, clothing and shelter . . ."

". . . they would turn up angels," interrupted the Prior. "My dear Martín, I am afraid you are wrong. You can give some people all the physical and material care in the world and still they turn out badly."

"I was not thinking only of physical and material care," said Martín quietly. "Of course that would not be enough. The boys and girls would have to have adequate supervision by people who would understand them and love them, and who could teach them and help them learn a trade and fit themselves for a good life. These supervisors should be people who do nothing else, who receive regular wages, and . . ."

"But, Martín, what are you thinking about? A regular staff! On a salary basis! It is unthinkable. It has never been done before. Where would the money come from?"

"I don't know. But it has to come. Father Prior, could I have your leave to talk this over with the Archbishop?"

Father Prior shook his head: "Martín, I can never make up my mind whether you suffer from a delusion of grandeur, or whether you are a s . . . Never mind. Go and see the Archbishop if you wish, though I am convinced it is perfectly useless."

The Archbishop approved the plan wholeheartedly, but, as the Prior had foreseen, he did not have the means to finance it. "Go and see the Viceroy," he suggested. "Perhaps His Most Christian Majesty's Government can do something."

Up to the palace of the Viceroy went Martín the Negro who used to clean toilets in the convent. In the midst of splendor and luxury he stood, quiet, unimpressed, determined. Centuries later, in India, another man, Gandhi, who also did not think it beneath him to do scavenging, would also stand, quiet, unimpressed and determined, in the palace of a viceroy. Speaking on behalf of people, men, women and children, victims of greed, both Martín and Gandhi sought the 'Kingdom of God and its justice.'

Having heard Martín's plea, the Viceroy threw up his hands. It was a fantastic project. After all, how could the Spanish Government be expected to look after everybody? Besides, if everyone would work, stick to their job . . . But people were shiftless, they wanted to get rich quick. And they did not go to church as they used to. Yes, that was the trouble: they did not go to church. If only the Archbishop would look into this . . . He, the Viceroy, could do nothing.

Back to the Prior went Martín. He was disappointed but he would not give up. "I guess I'll have to do it by myself."

"By yourself!" gasped the Prior. "Watch, Martín! You will fall into the sin of pride. What the convent, the Archbishop and the Viceroy cannot undertake, Martín de Porres will!"

"No, Father, not I, God will. May I be permitted to go on with my project?"

He was given permission and promptly started his campaign. He called personally on the wealthiest Spaniards. They told him they were already giving a considerable amount just to feed people. But Martín asked if it would not be better not to have so many people to feed in the near future because they themselves would have the means and the possibilities of making a living. Had not St. Augustine said: "You give bread to the hungry, but it would be better that there existed no one in need"? In order that boys and girls would grow into human beings capable of looking after themselves, the first requisite was to have them properly educated. No, Martín was not asking for alms. He was asking for justice. The conquistadors' wealth was ill-gotten through war and conquest. So it was the sheer duty of the rich Spaniards to make a restitution in the form of a home for homeless boys and girls. As a matter of fact, could they refuse to do so without endangering their own souls?

Martín's campaign was a huge success. The response was overwhelming. Money poured in. Everybody responded beyond expectation, and even the Archbishop and the Viceroy gave their support to the appeal. Within a few months, Martín had collected the equivalent in value of $400,000 dollars of our money.

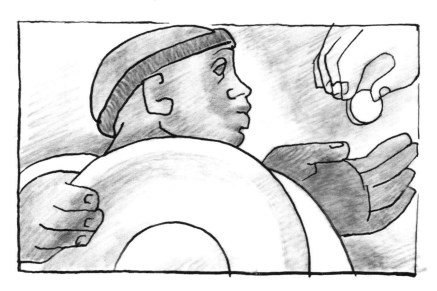

The home for boys and girls founded by Martín was the first of its kind in the New World. Not only was it run by a regular staff which included teachers, nurses (infirmarians as they were called), a chaplain, but it had also a resident physician. Boys were taught a trade, girls were taught all household duties and were presented with the required dowry. The home was opened to all, regardless of creed or race. Martín called it "Orphanage and School of the Holy Cross," and though it has changed buildings many times through the centuries, it still exists up to this day.

All in all Martín handled daily a considerable amount of money. Aside from the Boys' and Girls' Home, he helped weekly one hundred and sixty families or about one thousand people. He also collected money for the great number of humble priests who were starving, and also for Masses for the Souls in Purgatory. He also helped people who were in dire circumstances and too proud to ask. Martín would guess that they were in want and come secretly to their rescue. Every week also he collected money for shirts and blankets for destitute people, and also for toys and candy for children, and delicacies for old people and soldiers.

Such was his regular weekly round. It has been evaluated that in this way Martín distributed the equivalent of about $2000 of our money.

It seems that Martín distributed every week everything he had collected, saving nothing, but trusting God to fulfil the immediate needs and to take care of tomorrow's.

He himself never kept a cent, and therefore was occasionally hard put to meet an unexpected demand. For instance, one day he happened to go by the jail, and two men called him through the bars. They said they were very hungry and would Martín get them some bread. He did not have a cent and it was too far to go back to the convent kitchen. "Wait," he said, "I will be right back." He returned bring-

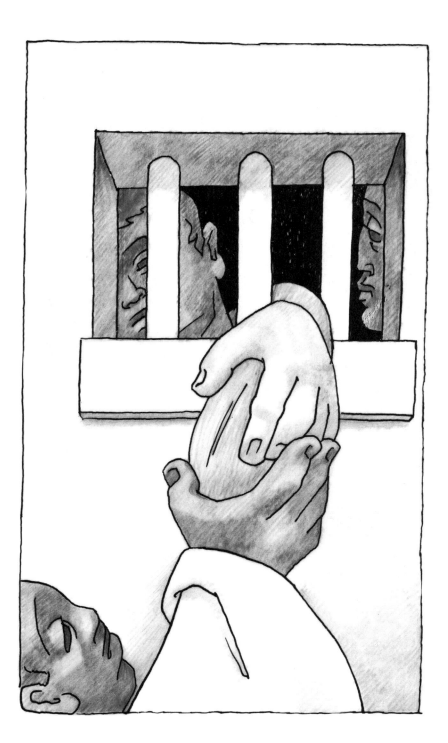

ing a loaf of bread. It was a very hot day. While devouring the bread one of the prisoners remarked:

"Eh, Brother, where is your hat? What did you do with that large hat of yours that you had a minute ago? You need it with that sun. Did you lose it?" Martín looked embarrassed, and the other prisoner noticed it. "I know!" he shouted. "I bet you had no money and you went and pawned that fine hat to buy us bread. Well, I declare, if I had met people like you before I would never have ended in jail."

It was the truth: Martín had pawned his hat. Several days later, his good friend Don Pastor came to the convent with the hat which he had spied in the window of the pawn shop as he went by.

"How did you know it was my hat?" asked Martín laughing.

"Who does not know Martín's hat in Lima?" retorted Don Pastor, laughing too.

He had pawned his hat for hungry prisoners, but there was nothing extraordinary in this. It was just part of the daily happenings. Didn't he know only too well what it was to be hungry? And did he not know what it was to be lonely, neglected, despised? His childhood memories were so vivid that he felt as if he were actually in the skin of the hungry and the rejected. He was the boy who wanted figs, and the one who stole because there was nothing to eat at home, and the rejected Indian, and the slave Negro, and the sick who could not afford medical care, and the old ones who had no place to go. He even knew how animals felt who were unwanted. Up to the end of his life he remained one with the little creatures of this earth and with the little people.

When the soldiers stationed in Callao used to see him coming every week down the dusty road with his basket full of delicacies for them, they greeted him as their faithful friend who did not hesitate to walk eight miles back and forth in the hot sun to bring them cheer. Martín had a way of making each person feel that he was the one foremost in Martín's thoughts; and so he was indeed, for the time being, precious above all else, unique.

Many people marveled at Martín's numerous enterprises. Just his medical activities alone would have filled the life of another person, especially since he was much sought after on account of his reputation for curing people. His very presence brought relief to sick people, and he was credited, in addition to medical knowledge, with what is called "healing hands." He himself never made such a claim, and on the contrary, always used his medical knowledge scrupulously in prescribing treatments and remedies. Then he left the cure in God's hands through prayer. Many of his patients made spectacular recoveries, and this continuously increased the demands for his help.

Yet, as we have seen, this work was but one of Martín's many activities. Each day was so full that we might well expect Martín to rush like mad from one thing to another. But we are told that he never gave the impression of being in a hurry. How did he do it?

FLYING BROTHER

THE "FLYING BROTHER," such was Martín's frequent nickname in Lima. At the time there were no planes and yet, over and over again, it is reported that he traveled to faraway places in an incredibly short time. In fact, no plane of ours can compete with his speed. According to testimonies, he was in several distant places at exactly the same time. One such testimony was told by a Spanish gentleman.

"I was made prisoner in Barbary.." (This country is called Algeria now, in North Africa.) "While I was held in bondage with other Christians, a Dominican Negro visited us, gave us medical care, talked to us and encouraged us by assuring us that we would recover our freedom. Indeed, later I was released and went back to Spain. Then I journeyed to Lima. One day I happened to pay a visit at the Dominican Convent and I was overjoyed when I suddenly recognized the Negro Dominican who had been so kind to us prisoners in Algeria. 'How are you?' I said to him. 'How wonderful to find you here. How was your trip back from Barbary?' These were simple enough questions, but I could not get any answer from Martín; he just made signs for me to keep quiet, and, later, when there were no people around he said to me that he did not wish anyone to speak about his trip to Africa. Now, this did not surprise me. It was just like him not to want anyone to know how kind he had been to us. But I could not remain silent forever, and one day, while he was gone to Limatambo, I told some other monks about Martín's work of mercy among the prisoners in Barbary. Whereupon they exclaimed: 'What? Martín in Barbary? But he has never left Peru, not even the convent, except for short walking trips to Limatambo or Callao!'"

Another day a young man visited the convent and he told about a remarkable Dominican he had met in Manila in the Philippines. Martín was much interested and said: "I wish I could meet him." Three days later the young man who had told the story met Martín again. Martín said quite naturally: "Ah! your friend, the Dominican of Manila, is well. He is very busy . . ." and Martín went on describing the Dominican's work in Manila and his surroundings with great detail. He even appeared to be familiar with the native language. He said all this in a very matter-of-fact way and, at the moment, he seemed totally unaware of how extraordinary his story sounded.

Again he did not seem to sense how strange it was when he prescribed an unknown remedy and astonished everybody by what he had to say about it. As the patient and those present did not seem inclined to take his prescription, he said casually: "I can assure you, it is going to relieve you. I have seen it used successfully in the hospital of Bayonne, in France."

Many other instances of Martín's ability to be in several distant places at the same time were reported, under oath, after his death. So were reported many stories of his being able, right in Lima, to be by the bedside of seriously ill patients attending to them, in spite of the bolted doors of houses and the fact that he was doing so without apparently leaving the convent.

All together, Martín, who spent all his religious life in Lima at the convent of the Holy Rosary, was reported to have made unaccountable trips to Africa, France, China, Japan and the Philippines and Mexico. This ability to do away with space and time is called ubiquity.

Not only was it reported that Martín had the gift of ubiquity, but he seems also to have had the gift of telepathy, the ability to read people's thoughts and see their unseen deeds. We came across one of the numerous instances of such power in connection with the false key of Juana and his patching up her quarrel with her husband.

Another time a group of novices went to have a chat with

Martín in his cell as they often did. When they arrived he
was not there. They sat around waiting. Then they began
to be bored and started rummaging around and opening
drawers. In one drawer they found some fruit which they
ate. Hearing Martín's footsteps they hurried back to their
seats as if nothing had happened. Martín came in and said
cheerfully: "Good! You have eaten the fruit. I left it in
the drawer for you." Then he turned to one of the students
and added evenly: "Now, give back that silver coin you
took from the drawer. It does not belong to you. It has an
owner." The student looked indignant: "I don't know what
you are talking about! I never took any silver coin from
your drawer!" he snapped. Martín said gently: "Come,
come! Take it out of your shoe. You put it there." Everybody was eagerly looking. The novice was very red as he
put his finger in his shoe and brought out the silver coin.

Martín had also the gift of prophecy; he could see way
ahead of time, sometimes years before, what was going to
happen to someone. As we already mentioned, he predicted
that little Brother Cypriano, of whom everyone made fun,
would become a fine-looking man and attain a high rank,
which he did.

He predicted also that the lay brother Ferdinando would
become a priest within fourteen years, which seemed most
improbable at the time, but it happened.

He predicted that his friend Don Juan de Figueroa, Governor of Lima, who was very ill, would not die at the time,
but would live for many more years. That he, Martín,
would die before the Governor. He added that the Governor
would be buried in the convent. "What?" cried the sick

Governor, "How could that be? A governor buried in a Dominican convent?"

"I can't help it," said Martín, "It will be so." It was. The Governor did recover from his illness as Martín had predicted. Many years later, after Martín's death, the Dominicans made a chapel out of Martín's cell and they asked the Governor to become patron of the shrine, and he accepted. Later, when the Governor died, he was buried next to Martín. Thus Martín's prophecy was fulfilled.

There are a great many reports of Martín's extraordinary gifts which cannot be explained because we do not know yet what kind of changes take place in the body of anyone who gives himself entirely to God as Martín did. Indeed, of all the wonders in Martín de Porres's astonishing life, the greatest of all is this love for God which filled all the hours of his days and nights.

As he rose at dawn to ring the convent bell, he offered his day to God. A busy time lay before him; a round of duties and tasks and a heavy burden of responsibilities.

During the day, people frequently noticed that he would be silent and quiet, just as if he were carrying on a conversation within himself. At first they said "What are you thinking about, Martín?" Then they understood that he was indeed carrying on a conversation within himself: he was talking to God. So they did not ask him anymore.

This talk to and with God was, to Martín, the most important part of his life. It remained the only thing he was absolutely sure he had to do. He had to keep this conversation going, and then, every thing else, work, tasks, duties, people would easily be attended to.

Because he never had enough time during the day to talk to God as much as he wanted, he reserved the greatest part of his nights for it. That is, instead of sleeping, he prayed and thought and meditated. He probably never slept more than three or four hours. Instead he talked to God, to Christ, to the Blessed Virgin whom he loved dearly.

He almost never slept in his own bed anyhow, but stretched on a board which was set in the Chapter hall, to receive dead bodies before funerals.

Once, when he was sick with the recurrent quaternary fever from which he suffered much every year, the Prior ordered him to put sheets on his own bed and sleep there. Martín put sheets on the bed, and slept there, only he did not undress but just lay on top of the covers. In that way he managed to obey the Prior and at the same time not to pamper himself.

The Prior always had a hard time to keep up with all Martín's doings and ideas. He was told that Martín scourged himself three times every night. This was what St. Dominic, the Founder of the Order, had done, and in those days scourging was part of the religious way of life. Nevertheless few practiced it, as least as severely as Martín did, therefore the Prior felt he had better question Martín about this. Martín was obviously annoyed at having been discovered, and he answered briefly: "It is true. I am doing voluntary penance for the people who do none. And God will make known all about these things when it pleases Him."

This and no more could the Prior learn from him. Martín did not feel he should talk about his penance, and it was only when he was dead that people discovered he wore a hair shirt directly on his flesh which was raw from the daily scourging. During his life nobody meeting him could have guessed that he was in such pain, so smiling, affable and untiring was he. It took heroic courage daily. But Martín was no molly-coddle. He was tough.

Martín never ate meat. Though he was scrupulously clean in his person he always wore an old habit.

He lived without any comfort for himself whatsoever. This was not because he despised the good things of this earth. He just had neither room nor time for them. He was too filled with concern for others and love of God, the two being inextricably bound together.

Of this he used to talk with his friend Juan Massias. Juan Massias was a Spaniard, younger than Martín, who had entered the convent of Santa María Magdalena. He too was inflamed with love for God and his fellow men. Martín used to pay him a monthly visit, and the two of them walked in the convent garden, side by side, telling each other about their plans and their thoughts. This was a real holiday for Martín and a great joy.

Among the most beautiful hours of Martín's life were the moments when he became so absorbed in his conversation with God that he did not know where he was. Several times, people entering the place where he was praying, reported they had seen Martín raised about one yard above ground, his eyes fixed on the crucifix. "Ah," used to say the Prior calmly, "if you keep around our Brother Martín long enough, you won't be surprised at anything."

These conversations with God, which sprang from his deep love, Martín carried on until the very end of his life. He was

sixty years old when Father Juan de Barbaran met him one day in the convent wearing a new habit instead of his usual old and mended one. "Why, Martín! How come you put on a new habit?"

"Oh," said Martín quietly, "this is the habit in which they will bury me."

Shortly after this he was taken ill. He had a high fever, and finally, the Prior persuaded him to get into bed. A doctor was called, but Martín told him that all remedies would be useless, and he foretold the day on which he would die.

As soon as the news of his illness spread in Lima, there was consternation and a great many people hastened to the convent. There was a crowd of poor people, Negroes, Indians and Spaniards, and also important dignitaries such as the Archbishop of Mexico who happened to be in Lima at the time and the Viceroy himself.

Upon being told that the Viceroy had arrived and wanted to see him, Martín said that the Viceroy should be asked to be kind enough to wait a while. After quite a time Martín had word sent that the Viceroy could come in. The Viceroy did, and falling upon his knees in front of Martín's bed, he begged him to pray for him who had such heavy responsibilities as Viceroy of Peru. Martín promised and the Viceroy left his cell only to find the entire convent ready to accompany him to his carriage with all the proper courtesy due the highest representative of the Spanish Government.

After he was gone the Prior hurried to Martín's bed and though he hated to do so, he thought it best to reprimand Martín for his behavior. "What in the world could legiti-

mate your keeping His Majesty's representative waiting?"
he asked sternly.

Martín said softly: "I was receiving great visitors at the
time."

"Great visitors!" exclaimed the Prior. "Who could be
greater in Peru than the Viceroy?"

"Our holy father St. Dominic, St. Catherine of Alexandria,
St. Vincent Ferrer, and the Blessed Virgin Mary," answered
Martín. "These heavenly visitors were here talking to me a

little while ago. That is the reason why I had to keep the
Viceroy waiting."

Martín's sufferings increased. All the Dominicans stood
around his bed, and the Archbishop of Mexico was there too.

They all recited the prayers for the dying.   Then they sang
the Credo. . . .

> "God of God, Light of Light . . ."

and as they came to the words

> "Et homo factus est"
> *And was made man*

Martín closed his eyes and died peacefully, on November
third, 1639.

PATRON OF SOCIAL JUSTICE 12

MARTÍN'S BURIAL was delayed for several days because of the great throng of people who flocked to see him from Lima and the countryside. They swarmed around his humble bed trying to touch his white and black habit. They cut many pieces of it and some people were reported cured of long-standing illnesses. Soon the habit was all torn, and twice the Dominicans had to replace it.

Everybody, whether poor or rich, Negro, white or Indian,

men, women, children, all said the same thing: "He was a saint." When it came to the burial ceremony, the Viceroy, the Archbishop of Mexico, the future Bishop of Cuzco and a Judge member of the Royal Chamber begged for the privilege of being pallbearers. And, though a humble lay brother, Martín was interred in the convent in a vault usually reserved for priests.

Inquiries for beatification purposes started as early as 1658. But Lima was far away from Rome and there were delays and shipwrecks. It was only in 1763 that Pope Clement XVIII proclaimed officially the heroism of Martín. And, in 1837, Pope Gregory XVI pronounced him beatified. On this occasion the Pope said that it was not because of his wonders, nor of his works, nor even of his sufferings, that the Church beatified Martín, but because he had been heroic in the practice of Christian virtues.

Martín was simple, straightforward, determined. He just saw what was needed and did it, no matter what seemed to be in the way at the time. He was several hundred years ahead of everybody in his understanding that before man is preached to about God, man needs to be fed, clothed, sheltered and educated.

It is not surprising that poor people started venerating Martín right after his death without even waiting for the official recognition of the Church. They knew he was on their side. He was and remains their friend. Neither bitter hardships nor excessive honors could ever wean Martín away from the oppressed, the exploited, the abandoned, the old and the sick.

Greedy and power-hungry people may have tried to use

Martín's name to quiet down their guilty consciences, or to strengthen their own privileges, by pointing out that Martín remained content all his life in an inferior position. What they forget is that Martín was given three times a choice whereby to achieve worldly recognition. By choosing the path of obscurity of his own free will, Martín was no different from many saints who also preferred the "little way." His three choices show that he could not be used by the mighty people to further their own ends.

Not only did he repeatedly disappoint ambitious people but he made matters quite uncomfortable for them by his quiet and firm conviction that nothing was too good for the poor and by acting accordingly.

Poor people and young people alike hail the undaunted spirit of Martín, his unconventional ways, his willingness to work out changes and improvements, his dashing and unpredictable boldness.

Martín's love for God remained inseparable from his love for men expressed through compassion and justice. And since now we are much concerned with justice the world over and with new ways of life, sixteenth-century Martín is very much up to date. Some of his ideas, like the one of communal orchards for the poor, are even ahead of the thinking of most people today. Therefore, though Martín had no political or social theory, it is most fitting that Peru has made him Patron of Social Justice. This was done in 1939 by the Government of Peru.

Saintly child of the New World in the first century of its conquest, Martín is a typical American in his way of getting things done quickly and efficiently, in his boundless enterprising spirit, in his strong feeling that a community has a duty toward all its people, and in his organization of medical care and educational facilities for all.

Martín is remembered also because he extended his eagerness to better human condition, regardless of color, race or creed.   And so, Martín was truly a peacemaker. More and more people are becoming aware of Martín's sanctity.   In 1951 the Pan-American Congress of Pharmacists selected Blessed Martín de Porres as their Patron, he who "regularly compounded drugs and preferred to use them as adjuncts to the healing of his presence." *   On this occasion Dr. Bedoya Villacorta spoke of Martín's love for the whole creation,

> ... from the lowly herb he used to prepare his remedies and in which he recognized the goodness of the Creator, to the timid rat and the raging bull, which to him were brothers also; from the degraded slave to the proud and conceited noble whom he doctored with equal care because he looked upon them as equal in the sight of the Creator and the Redeemer. Brother Martín, look down upon us who represent the pharmacists of Pan-America.   Free from all prejudice, we call upon you; we are taking you as our example, for you are the prototype of our professional ethics.   All of us who are here gathered together acclaim you as Patron of Pharmacy in America. **

* Reprinted with permission from an article entitled "A Patron For Pan-American Pharmacy", by Georgianna Simmons Gittinger, in *The Merck Report*, July 1951, published by Merck & Company, Inc., Rahway, New Jersey.

** Reprinted with permission from the translation of Dr. Bedoya Villacorta's speech by Father Norbert F. Georges, O.P., in his article entitled "Blessed Martín de Porres," *The Torch* (October, 1952).

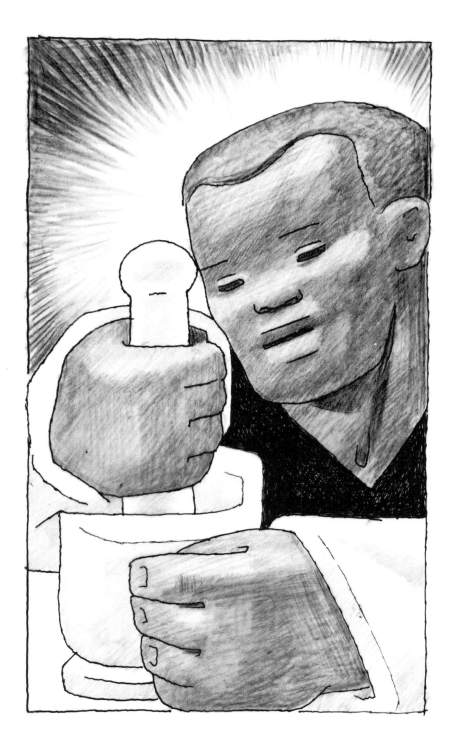

Martín's feast day is on November fifth. There are relics, statues and medals which can be found at The Blessed Martín Guild in New York. Martín is especially venerated in Friendship Houses, all over the United States, where people meet as friends regardless of financial condition, race or creed.

All of us can carry Martín in our hearts as a great and dear friend. Then he may teach us how to surrender ourselves to God so completely that we serve all men best.

Thus we will follow in the footsteps of Martín de Porres, a tough spiritual giant who towers above average mankind, a member of the heroic vanguard of those who are truly Christlike.

DATE DUE

OCT 23 '78	OCT 18 '78		
GAYLORD			PRINTED IN U.S.A.